jade goody

goody

story of a survivor

neil simpson

JOHN BLAKE

Published by John Blake Publishing Ltd,
3 Bramber Court, 2 Bramber Road,
London W14 9PB, England

www.blake.co.uk

First published in paperback in 2006

ISBN 1 84454 270 X

British Library Cataloguing-in-Publication Data:

A catalogue record for this book is available from the British Library.

Design by www.envydesign.co.uk

Printed in Great Britain by Bookmarque

1 3 5 7 9 10 8 6 4 2

Papers used by John Blake Publishing are natural, recyclable products made
from wood grown in sustainable forests. The manufacturing processes conform
to the environmental regulations of the country of origin.

Every attempt has been made to contact the relevant copyright-holders,
but some were unobtainable. We would be grateful if the appropriate people
could contact us.

For everyone who has ever made it into the
Big Brother house.

Contents

chapter 1

And the Winner is...

'Alex, Jade, Jonny and Kate. You are down to the final four. The phone lines are closed. The votes have been counted and verified, and I can reveal that the ninth person to leave the Big Brother house will be –'

Looking directly into the camera, *Big Brother* host Davina McCall began one of the most famous, longest and most awful pauses in live television. Less than 400 yards away, over a barbed-wire fence and inside the *Big Brother* compound, the four survivors of Series 3 sat close together on the orange sofas, unable to speak and hardly breathing.

More seconds passed. More tension mounted. More than 10 million people watching the show at home or following events live on the Internet were waiting for the moment to end. Then Davina yelled out just one word: 'Jade!'

Nearly two thousand people in the crowd all around Davina erupted. There were cheers, jeers, screams and shouts. Channel 4 later said that the noise outside Elstree TV and Film Studios could be clearly heard more than two miles away in built-up Barnet. And Davina hadn't finished. 'Jade. You have got one minute to say your goodbyes. I'm coming to get you!' she yelled as the crowd got even wilder.

And so, after nine long weeks, Jade Goody, the 21-year-old from Bermondsey in South-East London, had come fourth in *Big Brother*. Later that evening, trainee solicitor Kate Lawler would be crowned the official winner of the 2002 contest – the first time a woman had collected the £70,000 top prize.

But Jade would turn out to be the real winner of the show. Kate, and almost every other *Big Brother* contestant before and since, has now pretty much faded from public view. But Jade is still very much in the spotlight. And she is also in the money.

The former dental nurse from a broken home in one of London's poorest boroughs, savagely mocked and derided by television and the tabloids, has ended up laughing all the way to the bank.

Within little more than a year of leaving the show that made her famous, Jade became Britain's first reality-TV millionaire. Two years on and her earning power shows no sign of letting up. At the end of 2004, she collected £30,000 for less than three weeks' work in Channel 4's *Big Brother Panto*, for example. All the other former contestants from previous *Big Brother*s had to make do with just £5,000. Jade is also continuing to collect a six-figure income from magazine and newspaper interviews and columns. She has invested in property, helps run one beauty business in Essex and is planning to launch a second. Despite a critical mauling, her fitness videos are still selling well. She has starred in an impressive number of top-rated TV programmes and has several more equally lucrative new projects in the pipeline.

Financial experts say no other star from any of Britain's other reality-TV shows has even come close to Jade's earning power. Or her staying power. So just who is Jade Goody and how has she succeeded where so many other television wannabes have failed?

At 8.30 p.m. on Saturday, 27 July 2002, Jade was just a frightened 21-year-old about to face the public after nine weeks of booze- and argument-fuelled isolation in the *Big Brother* house. Terrified, she hugged Alex, Jonny and Kate to say goodbye, and pulled her silver suitcase behind her as she climbed the 18 steps that would lead her back to reality. 'I'm so scared,' was all she could say before leaving the house. 'So scared. I'm shaking like a leaf.'

'You'll be fine, just smile, we'll see you in a few minutes,' shouted Kate, supportive at last. And then they all heard the final booming instruction: 'Jade. Please leave the *Big Brother* house.' The disembodied voice echoed through the Elstree studio – but Jade didn't know how to get out. In a final and completely typical moment of madness, she couldn't work out how to open the door. 'Jade. Please leave the *Big Brother* house,' came the instruction again while she started to laugh hysterically, turning back towards her three former housemates and pushing and pulling each of the two doors in turn. The crowd was yelling even louder and the booming instruction came a third time, before an assistant on the outside of the house edged one of the doors open to show Jade where to go.

Then, finally, Jade Goody was free. The cool early-evening air blew her blonde hair across her face as she stared open-mouthed at the crowds. In theory she was back in the real world. But the scenes ahead of her were like nothing she had ever seen before.

Jade was standing on a high metal platform on the edge of the gleaming white *Big Brother* compound. It was the same spot where she had been briefly frisked more than two months earlier when she had first entered the house as an anonymous 20-year-old – the youngest housemate in the history of the show.

Since then Jade, entirely unknown to her, had become both the most hated and the most loved woman in Britain. Statistically speaking, she had temporarily become the most famous woman in Britain as well. Media analysts found that, in the summer of 2002, more newspaper column inches were devoted to stories about Jade than to anyone else, including the Queen. And it was Her Majesty's Golden Jubilee year.

'I can't believe it. Can't believe it,' Jade repeated again and again to herself as she clutched at her dress and tried to find her bearings. In front of her on eviction night were two black-clad security guards, both holding walkie-talkies and telling her to move forwards, down the shiny metal staircase, through the barbed-wire-covered gate, down more stairs and on to a second metal platform.

Jade, however, could hardly see a thing. Harsh white lights from the vast gantries above her sucked the life out

4

of her cheeks. Camera flash bulbs from down below were dazzling her, cutting like strobes into her eyes, recording every excited, terrified expression, every nervous smile, every scream of relief.

Suddenly, though, Jade did see something – *Big Brother* host Davina McCall was on the first metal platform, rushing forward for a hug. 'I am so excited,' Davina yelled to the cameras, as she grabbed the former housemate and tried to lead her off the steps and into the centre of the crowd. But Jade had other ideas. A huge group of photographers, standing three-deep on either side of the stairway, were yelling at her and demanding that she posed for pictures. Unsure of what to do, Jade obliged. She smiled, laughed, threw out her hands and tried to remember every second of this once-in-a-lifetime experience.

Davina, meanwhile, had a schedule to follow and an important message to get across. 'I always feel very protective of the housemates when they come out as they're very vulnerable then,' says Davina, who was then in her third year as *Big Brother* host. She knew few were as vulnerable as 21-year-old Jade and she was desperate to tell her not to worry about the occasional boos and jeers that were coming out of some parts of the crowd. If she had had time, Davina would have told her to ignore some of the less flattering banners that fans of rival housemates had unfurled as well.

Fortunately, Jade was too wrapped up in the moment to care, to hear the catcalls or to see the cruel slogans. 'I could hear people yelling out, "Jade, you're a minger," but I just tried to tell myself that I was in fact a winner just to be there on a night like this,' she admitted bravely once the ordeal was over.

Meanwhile, this was live television and Davina wanted to pull Jade on to the eye-shaped *Big Brother* stage and into the studio for what was going to be one of the most raucous, laughter-filled and frequently interrupted eviction interviews of the series.

'Come on, Jade, come on, let's meet the rest of your adoring public,' Davina called as the first of several pairs of boxer shorts were thrown over the heads of the crowd and landed in Jade's arms. Shaven-headed minders followed the women closely as they edged across the tarmac and climbed the next set of steps on to the stage. 'They love her,' Davina yelled at the cameras, trying to drown out some more occasional jeers in the crowd. 'Now go to the middle and enjoy it,' she told a still terrified Jade.

The crowd roared again as Jade did just that. She was wearing her favourite dress, an extravagant, strapless, pale-pink satin number with matching sleeves and diamante details. It would have been an ideal choice for a fancy dinner party, a night in an expensive restaurant or maybe cocktails in a trendy bar. However, it wasn't so ideal for climbing up flights of stairs while dragging a suitcase, running across high-level metal walkways, being grabbed by screaming fans or trying to hug a dozen people at once. And, as Jade had been doing all of these things, the inevitable had started to happen. 'Her boobs are about to pop out,' cried Davina, as Jade yelled her thanks to the crowd.

'You're all chipsticks. Thank you! Thank you so much!' Jade screamed through Davina's microphone before being dragged off the stage, past another crowd of fans and round the corner to Elstree's vast George Lucas sound stage, where the *Big Brother* producers worked and where the live eviction interviews were filmed.

The tough, time-consuming walk from the house doors to the studio was a deliberate ploy on the part of *Big Brother* designers. This was the first year the house hadn't been built on the marshes of Bow, East London, so it was the first year that evicted housemates hadn't had to walk over the famous bridge back to freedom. 'We knew we couldn't replicate the bridge they had to cross at Three Mills,' said series editor Gigi Eligoloff in the official *Inside Big Brother* book. 'But we couldn't have any old walk instead with the studio 10 ft from the house. There has to be some sense of making a journey from the cloistered world of the *Big Brother* house back to their old life, with the audience throwing reality into their faces. There has to be the moment when they are caught like a startled deer in the headlights as all the press photographers' flashes go off – a chance to be momentarily reunited with friends and family before being whisked into the studio by Davina.'

Jade, uniquely, had more than just friends and family to see inside the studio – as Davina was desperately trying to tell her. 'Jade, somebody amazing is here to see you with your mum. We've got a celebrity. A celebrity who is your biggest fan,' she yelled. But still Jade held back, mesmerised by the crowds, the noise, the music and the excitement. 'It's not easy to get Jade to leave somewhere,' Davina admitted to the cameras, giving the housemate one final pull as they approached the studio, walking quickly past one anti-Jade banner shaped like a giant pig's head.

On the threshold of the massive sound stage, there was a final burst of confusion. 'Jade, go see your mum; your mum's there,' Davina cried out. But Jade couldn't see her. She couldn't get her eyes to adjust to the relative darkness of the studio after the glare and the camera flashes from outside. Then, suddenly, she saw her mum Jackiey run towards her and leaped forward to grab the blonde, black-clad figure. Jumping up and down and starting to cry, Jade reached out for all her other friends as well. They had been apart for more than two months, unable to see each other, to speak on the phone or even to send a text message. Being back in the real world suddenly felt fantastic, though things were about to get unreal again pretty fast.

'Jade! Jade – look!' Davina played her winning card and led a sleeveless, red-shirted Graham Norton into the scrum. Jade was dumbstruck for an instant. This was the man she had listed on her original *Big Brother* application form as her favourite comedian but whom she had never expected to actually meet. 'Oh my God!' she shrieked, falling into the chat-show host's arms. 'Hello! It's my Jader, my Jader!' Graham replied, understandably thinking he would be the focus of all her attention. But then something amazing, touching and entirely unexpected happened. The very moment Jade reached out to hug Graham she spotted her grandmother and grandfather waiting quietly in the wings. And she wanted to hug and hold them even more.

Graham Norton, the millionaire king of the late-night

chat-show circuit, was effectively pushed aside as the previously unknown dental nurse proved that her priorities and her loyalties still lay with her family and friends. For all the madness and confusion around her, the Bermondsey girl certainly hadn't forgotten her roots.

To his credit, Graham handled the unexpected rejection well. He carried on clapping and smiling in the background as Jade moved on from her grandparents not back to him but to the friends she had spotted on the other side of the studio's entrance. And then Davina was back in control. The show had to go on and after the three-minute commercial break it was time for the big interview. Davina pulled Jade aside for an important pep talk.

'I always give housemates a chance to redeem themselves in the interviews,' she said. 'So when they get booed I will say in the ad break before we talk, "Look, they're booing you because of this. I'm going to ask you some questions about it and you've got plenty of time and a good chance to redeem yourself." It wouldn't be fair to do things any other way.'

Jade may not have heard all the boos or jeers that had accompanied her journey out of the house so far that evening. But as she had been the target of an unprecedented hate campaign in the media, she had more need than most of redemption. And as a huge fan of Jade, Davina was determined to earn it for her. 'I'm quite soppy about Jade,' she said when the final day's filming was over. 'What the press don't look at when they are being anti-Jade is where she has come from and what has made her like that, and why she may not have gone to school for as long as she could have done. You know, Jade has had a really tough life but nobody wants to look at that. She needs love. She craves the smallest bit of attention and when she gets it she turns into a little girl.'

Davina's colleague Dermot O'Leary, the host of *Big Brother's Little Brother* who was waiting to meet Jade immediately after her first live interview, agreed. 'Everything Jade does makes me wet myself. Every now and then she just reverts to being a five-year-old and you just have to love her for it,' he said.

And everyone was going to love Jade's post-eviction interview. By the time the commercial break was over, Jade and Davina were sitting on the stylish yellow chairs in the centre of the sound stage. The vast open room, where key scenes from the *Star Wars* epics had been filmed, resembled a giant aircraft hangar or superstore. Studio lights shone down from gantries high above and television screens of all sizes beamed live and recorded pictures of the *Big Brother* house from every angle. Finally, behind the crowd control barriers were the fans – including Jade's family, friends and former housemates.

'Were you surprised at that reception? Were you worried that you wouldn't be loved?' asked a delighted Davina, getting started on the interview she said she had been looking forward to since the first day of the series on 24 May.

'I was really nervous, I couldn't believe it, thanks so much,' was all an overwhelmed Jade could say. 'I had heard horrible things over the wall. Horrible. I didn't know what to expect. I was frightened. I was gutted…' She trailed off, her face in her hands.

But Davina had another trick up her sleeve, another way to prove to Jade that she didn't need to worry any more, because another celebrity fan was about to be unveiled. The face of Hollywood star Johnny Depp suddenly appeared on the vast bank of television screens above Jade's head. He was being interviewed for breakfast television show *RI:SE* to promote his latest film, *Lost in La Mancha*, and *Big Brother* had come up in conversation.

'They've been slagging off that poor girl and I want her to win, bless her heart,' Johnny said in the interview before looking directly at the camera. 'Jade should win. Good luck, Jade.'

Tears started to fall down her face again and the 21-year-old motormouth from Bermondsey was, just for a moment, speechless. Just what had been going on while she had been in the *Big Brother* house? She couldn't remember any contestant in either of the previous shows getting a Hollywood heavyweight on their side in their eviction interviews. As the cameras continued to roll, Jade started to realise just how much her life had changed – though Depp wasn't to be her last film-star supporter. Years later she was on a plane and got talking to anglophile and *Pulp Fiction* star Samuel L Jackson. They got on well. Jade asked him for an autograph and he told her off for drinking too much – because he had recognised her and had just seen the latest set of embarrassing pictures of her leaving a nightclub after a few too many drinks.

Back in 2002, however, Davina had had some equally tough home truths to offer Jade. 'This was the most bitchy *Big Brother* to date,' she said. 'And, Jade, I have to say, you were kind of at the centre of it. Let's just have a look at this.'

Then, on every television screen in the studio, Jade had to watch and hear herself tear into every one of her fellow housemates. It was sobering stuff and Jade was desperate to explain herself. 'I know I look like I'm an awful person, but I'm not,' she began.

But Davina interrupted. 'Everyone in the house said you were two-faced, Jade. But you always said that whatever you said behind someone's back you also said to their face. So we trawled through the cuttings and we found out –' Davina again paused for effect – 'that you were telling the truth.'

The screens suddenly filled with a second montage of clips, where Jade quietly told the individual housemates all the things she had said to the others in anger on other occasions. Jade, who had been demonised as a two-faced, back-stabbing super-bitch, had finally been publicly vindicated. So she started to cry yet again.

Experts say it is impossible to retain any sense of time when you are being interviewed amid such extreme circumstances on live television. So Jade could be excused for hoping that her moment in the spotlight was about to draw to a close at this point. Surely all Davina had left to show was her 'best bits' compilation then she could go for a proper catch-up with her mum and friends? Davina, of course, had other plans.

Did Jade, or did she not, give PJ a BJ under the *Big Brother* duvet? It was the question that the whole country had been asking since the drunken night in Week 2 of the show had pushed the series to the top of the ratings. And Davina was right there to ask it.

'I got drunk, it was stupid, it was embarrassing. If I go out there and Davina puts it on the big screen, I wouldn't know what to say. But I know it could be mentioned,' Jade had said to Adele back in the house when she had been asked if she had any regrets about her time on the show. *Could be mentioned?* You bet it could, Jade. It had transfixed the country for most of the summer, after all. So Jade put her face in her hands and mouthed, 'I'm sorry, so sorry,' again and again as the famous clip went up on the big screen as well.

The audience went wild and Davina wasn't going to let it drop. As it was before the evening watershed and children were deemed to be watching, she wasn't able to discuss the fumbles with Jade in much detail. So Davina and the production staff had come up with another strategy. 'Which base did you get to?' she asked, coming round to crouch next to Jade and showing her a list of four possible sex acts written on her cue card.

Fingers shaking, blushing wildly and laughing almost uncontrollably, Jade pointed to one of the four choices and whispered that she would tell Davina more in private. For her part, Davina, fully aware of her audience, said she would tell all as soon as they had passed the watershed in half an hour. The audience went wild again – and one voice in particular rang out above all the others. At first Davina had thought they were being interrupted by Jade's mum Jackiey, and she laughingly shouted her down. But then Davina realised it was someone else.

'That's Avid, your other number-one fan,' she said as

13

another cry of 'I love you, Jade' echoed round the studio. 'He's come out of the woodwork since *Big Brother* has been on.' Channel 4's Avid Merrion, the alter ego of comedian Leigh Francis, had just launched *Bo' Selecta!*, in which he took on the role of key female celebrities' 'superfans'. Jade, and indeed Davina, were going to see a whole lot more of him in the coming months.

In the meantime, Davina wanted to show everyone a whole lot more of Jade. All of her, to be exact. Cue a repeat of Jade's drunken strip after losing the word-association game the housemates had played on Day 47. What had possessed her to go through with the challenge? Davina asked.

'I didn't think for a minute that I'd be the only bird naked on the settee,' was all Jade could think of to say, blushing again and her face firmly back in her hands. The interview seemed to be lasting for ever and Jade's public embarrassment was far from over. 'Next we get to the moment that we felt defined you in the house,' teased Davina. It was verucca-gate, and Jade looked up in horror as she watched herself screech and scream round the living room in her underwear, infamously laying into 'this minging, dirty *BB* house'.

Then, and only then, could Jade relax and see what the *Big Brother* producers had put together as her 'best bits'. On screen she saw her hair-dye disaster, her wild dancing, her fancy-dress evenings, her spaceman routine. She saw herself eat, eat and eat – then complain about being hungry. She saw herself trapped in the Diary Room, splitting her favourite trousers, trying vainly and hilariously to exercise, flirting and worse with PJ, running around the garden and falling down every few minutes. And she heard her favourite phrase – chipstick, chipstick, chipstick. It was how she would like to be remembered, she told Davina before being led back outside to the darkening evening and the excited fans.

'Here she is! It's Jade!' Davina yelled as they left the studio to an ever-bigger roar from the crowd. The boos, at last, had stopped and Jade was finally getting the genuine applause she deserved. 'I don't think she can quite believe it,' Davina said, watching the tearful youngster climb back on to the main *Big Brother* stage to acknowledge her fans. It had been an incredible start to the final day of the 2002 series.

Jade had collected 1,404,422 votes, just over 20 per cent of the total number polled – an amazing result for someone who had languished at the bottom of every Internet popularity chart for the first few weeks of the show and had been savagely attacked by the media for much of the series. Later that evening, Alex, Jonny and then Kate would follow in Jade's footsteps as the show drew to a close. But, for all the excitement of their evictions and of Kate's ultimate victory, it was clear to everyone that Jade was the real winner that evening.

'Jade has the magic formula,' said legendary publicist Max Clifford. 'She is a breath of fresh air and the one person I think could genuinely become a star from this programme. She should be a millionaire within a year.' As usual, Max was right. But Jade's life could have been very, very different.

Big Brother's youngest entrant and biggest winner had to

fight every step of the way, from a fractured childhood through a troubled adolescence and a high profile coming of age. She was still to find out just how brutal the press and the public had been about her looks and her behaviour in the house. And she was unaware of just how many awful kiss-and-tell stories about her were yet to be printed.

On the night of Jade's eviction, her thoughts about the future were surprisingly modest. 'I just want to have fun with my girlfriends,' she said. 'My idea of a good time is having a night in with the girls, a bottle of wine, a video and painting our toenails.' The extraordinary new schedule the *Big Brother* producers and Jade's newly acquired show business advisers were putting together meant it was going to be quite a while before she could have a quiet night in like this again, however.

When she got over the hurt and the headlines, Jade was going to put her head down and work hard at making a success of her moment in the spotlight. She would do whatever it took to carve out a well-paid career in the media and leave her past behind. She would become a fixture on London's glamorous party and première circuit. And she was going to love every minute of it.

'Is there any downside to being famous?' she was asked six months after *Big Brother* ended.

Jade couldn't think of one. 'I enjoy it all,' she said honestly. 'I don't find anything difficult about it. If I had to say just one thing that was bad, it would be that I can't go out without any blusher on any more. I can't just run out to the shops in my pyjamas. But I can hardly complain about that.'

And the fact that Jade never did complain about the way the media treated her was part of her long-term appeal. She put up with attacks and criticism that would have destroyed many other people, and carried on bouncing back. It made her strong. It made her friends. And it helped her defy all the odds.

'On previous experience, *Big Brother* is a factory for has-beens. All contestants are pretty much forgotten after a few months, but this notorious motormouth from the third series clearly thinks she will be different,' proclaimed the *Daily Telegraph* dismissively the day after the series ended in 2002.

But what the newspaper didn't know was that Jade *was* going to be different. She had been for years. Her troubled, tortured childhood had seen to that.

chapter 2

Bermondsey Girl

If the scriptwriters of EastEnders had wanted to conjure up the cliché of a dysfunctional, disadvantaged, working-class family, they could have done worse than to look just south of the River Thames to the Goody family in Bermondsey, South-East London.

There, in a council house in one of the country's poorest boroughs, they would have found a grandmother who had been shoplifting for more than a quarter of a century; a father who had been in and out of prison; a brother who had been adopted at birth, taken abroad and rarely spoken about since; and a partially disabled mother.

And at the centre of it all they would have found a loud, mouthy daughter who bunked off school to look after her mum, got into trouble, got bullied and looked set to repeat the bad patterns of all the generations before her. They would have found Jade Goody.

As one commentator said, when *Big Brother* had just ended, you can forget the Osbournes. If you want a really wild, damaged family then meet the Goodys.

Jade Cerisa Lorraine Goody was born on 5 June 1981 when her mum Jackiey was just 21 years old. She was Jackiey's second child. The first, Brett, had been adopted as a baby five years earlier. He had moved to Australia with his new family, though even there he wasn't safe from the tabloid reporters wanting to dig some dirt on his half-sister when she hit the headlines in *Big Brother*.

But this time around Jackiey was determined to keep her healthy baby girl. She hadn't been with her new partner, Andy, for very long and at 18 he was even younger than she was. But Jackiey wanted a settled, conventional family life. She was sure that she and Andy could make their stormy relationship work and build a loving home for their baby.

Unfortunately for all of them, she was wrong. Happy families in the Goody household lasted less than two years before the rows and threats of violence got out of control, and Andy stormed out. It was not long before he was back in trouble with the police and facing the first of his many stretches in prison.

It meant Jade and her mum were left to look after themselves in one of the very roughest parts of town. Today much of Bermondsey has been smartened up. Flash apartment blocks have been carved out of the old derelict warehouses in its narrow streets. Dress designer Zandra Rhodes picked it for the site of her bright-pink Fashion and Textile Museum and by the river there are some of London's most expensive restaurants – including Le Pont de la Tour, where Tony and Cherie Blair famously took Bill and Hillary Clinton to dinner in 1997. But all that was still to come when Jade was out playing in the mean streets there as a child. 'It was run-down and rough,' she says. 'But you have to make the most of what you've got and I didn't really have an unhappy time of growing up. My mum certainly did her best.'

And for a while it looked as if the two of them would survive just fine with Andy out of the picture. Jackiey says Jade was a happy, ebullient child – always smiling and ready to sing, dance and put on a show. One day the pair went to a local council festival where Jade, still a child, ended up on stage trying to join in while others performed songs and routines from the show *Fame*. She says it was one of her favourite memories of childhood. And it could have led to so much more.

At five, Jade got a bit part as an extra in the television series *London's Burning* and loved meeting and getting autographs from all the actors and crew. She wasn't particularly articulate, and her South-East London accent was pretty much as impenetrable then as it is today. But she and Jackiey still thought she could maybe use acting or performing as a stepping stone to a better life. Plenty of other child stars before Jade had made more money than their parents had ever dreamed of and lifted their whole families out of poverty in the process.

But Jade's faltering career as a child actress was never to get off the ground. She came home from a friend's flat one day to find tearful neighbours crowding round, waiting to give her some tragic news. It turned out that her mum had been out riding pillion on her brother Martin's motorcycle – and there had been a terrible accident.

Martin, just 19 and Jade's favourite uncle, was dead by the time the ambulance was able to get him to hospital for treatment. Meanwhile, Jackiey had been taken to the intensive care unit of Guy's Hospital near London Bridge Station, where she was fighting for her life.

And there was an even more extraordinary family tragedy just round the corner. By a cruel twist of fate Jackiey was now in the same hospital where Jade's much-loved great-grandmother Martha, 86, was being treated for terminal throat cancer. The old lady died within hours of being told that her son was dead, that her daughter was only clinging to life and that her great-granddaughter was crying desperately downstairs in the visitors' room.

It is impossible to know what Jade went through that day and how it would affect her for the rest of her life. Can anything be much worse than losing two close family members and seeing your mother unconscious and partially paralysed, all in the same day, when you are just five years old? Jade says that even now she can hardly speak of the incident.

'I'll never forget being brought into the hospital and being told my mum might die. My favourite uncle had died and now my nan was about to die too.' Her voice falters and she can't and won't talk about it any more.

As luck would have it, Jackiey did pull through, but she was suffering from a broken neck and a broken collarbone. She now had one blind eye and a paralysed left arm that would never fully recover. After some minor operations

Jackiey was moved to a different hospital in London – and she remained there, needing constant care for nearly two years. It left five-year-old Jade in limbo.

'With Dad back in prison I went from relative to relative to be looked after,' says Jade, quietly and sadly. 'For the first nine months Mum was pretty much out of it. I'd sit by her bedside and chat away, but things were really bad as Mum had so many hospital drugs in her. She even forgot me at one point. She forgot that she had a daughter because her memory had been affected by the accident.'

It was the hardest possible upbringing. And it was about to get even worse. When Jade was seven years old, her mother finally came home from hospital, even though she could hardly care for herself, let alone for her daughter. And with Andy out of the picture and back in prison, there was only one person to hold the household together. That person was Jade herself.

Still at primary school, Jade was forced to take on the role of her mother's main carer, which was effectively a 24-hours-a-day, seven-days-a-week job. 'I had to wash her, shave her armpits, do her hair for her. It was hard but because it's your mum you don't mind,' she says, admitting that apart from anything else the experience dramatically affected her ability to make and keep friends locally. 'I was only young so I had to learn to cook, clean, iron and even wire plugs. Of course there were times when it was so hard. Other girls would be out playing after school but I'd be up until 3 a.m. sometimes, doing mum's hair and stuff. I'd also have to dress her and wash her in the mornings.' Again Jade has to cut interviews short when she is asked how she and Jackiey coped. They are dark times she wants to put behind her. Filed away and never discussed, if not ever fully forgotten.

Yet Jade is happy to talk about how all this had an impact on her education – because she knows this can help raise awareness of the problems so many other young carers face across the country.

Today Jade is a passionate supporter of the work unpaid carers do across the country. Her life story was used as the basis of a radio report into 'kids who care' on Five Live and is credited with raising vital awareness of the plight of so many families who quietly get each other through the worst that life can throw at them. She also nominated children's charity NCH, formerly known as the National Children's Home, as one of the three she would like to receive her share of the jackpot if she won the *Back To Reality* TV show in 2004.

NCH was then running a campaign to raise the amount of support available to people going through what Jade had endured a decade and a half earlier. 'Young carers face serious responsibilities,' says the charity, which estimates there could be at least 15,000 youngsters looking after parents or siblings across the country. 'In addition to the daily tasks they complete for their parents such as housework, cooking and bathing, they live with the added pressure of school and often a lack of understanding from schoolmates. The physical and emotional strain is sometimes too much – many young carers skip school and suffer depression.'

The words could have been written to describe the plight of young Jade Goody.

'Sometimes at school I'd be so worn out that I'd fall asleep at the desk,' she said. 'Even when I was awake I couldn't concentrate on lessons because Mum was always on my mind and I worried about her. I missed quite a bit of school because of Mum – and because of that I wouldn't know about a few things like geography or history or a few famous people like Mother Teresa. Sometimes I couldn't take it in because I was so tired.'

And that's not surprising because Jade didn't just have to look after her mother in the evenings. Sometimes she found she couldn't control her in the daytime either. Jackiey has admitted that she once lashed out at Jade's primary school head teacher, in a row about something no one really remembers. It was hardly behaviour that would endear a child to her teachers. So Jade's faltering education continued to be disrupted from all sides.

In her defence, Jade was not alone in falling behind educationally. Despite the very best efforts of the borough's army of teachers and support staff, the proportion of local school leavers getting five or more GCSE grades still stands at less than 30 per cent. The national average is nearly 48 per cent. And Jade was hardly helped by the wider economic situation in her neighbourhood.

Southwark was then, and continues to be, one of the most disadvantaged areas of London, let alone Britain. Unemployment in the area currently stands at around 9 per cent. That's more than double the figure for the rest of London. In the smaller area of Rotherhithe, where Jade went to school, the figure is currently 12 per cent – nearly triple the London average.

Figures show that some 40 per cent of children are raised in lone-parent families and 42 per cent grow up in a home where there is no working adult. At any one time a minimum of 60 per cent of adults in Southwark rely on some degree of state benefits to survive – and the borough is currently eighth in the national index of deprivation compiled by the Department of the Environment, Transport and the Regions.

Regrettably, the Goody household was typical of many of the troubled homes in the area. And for Jade there always seemed to be a new nightmare just round the corner that would push her even further behind. When she was eight, for example, her mum was cooking dinner one evening and wasn't aware that her hand was in the frying pan. 'She had no feeling in it,' says Jade, 'so she just carried on cooking, even though it was burning badly.'

A little later there was an even worse incident. The Goodys were trying to save money by using candles rather than electric lights – yet both of them had fallen asleep. 'A candle melted to the end and set fire to the wardrobe,' says Jade. 'By the time I woke up the flames were leaping up. It was horrible. I remember screaming to try and wake Mum up. She was left-handed and she'd lost her left hand so it was difficult for her to move much at the time. I don't know how I did it but I dragged her out of bed and somehow managed to carry her outside through all the flames and smoke. She was about three times bigger than me and I was starting to panic. I was just a kid, not even 10, and I had to use all my strength. I can still feel the heat of the flames in our bedroom. Then we were outside and safe.'

Neighbours recall being amazed at how well the nine-year-old girl coped with this awful situation. And how determined she was to ensure that her mum avoided any blame for the incident. Her home life was far from ideal. But Jade didn't want it broken up any further by well-meaning social workers who might have thought it was better to split up the fractured family for good and put her into care.

With so much going on, it is little wonder that Jade and her mum argued as well. 'Daughters are always going to have arguments with their mums, but it was worse for me because there was a lot of frustration there. Mum would shout and then break down and cry with guilt because she knew I was only trying to help. I had to learn from a very young age that you have to be understanding,' says Jade, uncharacteristically quietly.

And in the powder-keg atmosphere of the Goody household at that time even the smallest of these arguments could erupt into something far bigger.

'It made Mum very frustrated that she couldn't do things for herself,' Jade admits. 'I'd be doing her hair and suddenly she'd start shouting and screaming at me. Just once, in a real temper, she hit me because I hadn't fixed my Wendy house properly. I was black and blue. I had to go to school that day and I was having trouble sitting down so the teachers knew things weren't right. Mum told me later that she rang Social Services to say that she was scared that she'd hit me again. She told them she just couldn't cope and asked them to take me away because she was worried she was ruining my life. She actually wanted them to put me on a risk list. I now know that Social Services decided not to do that – and I'm so glad. Mum and me are a team. We're a family.'

Jackiey was soon to learn that, far from ruining her daughter's life, she was actually in a good position to make her stronger. But first of all she had to persuade the youngster that a good education was worth having – and that school was a serious place. Looking back, Jade recognises that she pushed her luck with more bad behaviour than was strictly necessary.

'I certainly missed a lot of primary school because of caring for Mum,' she says. 'Then, come secondary school, I'd be rebellious. I'd be the one who stopped everyone from working by talking. My mates used to talk and work but I couldn't do both at the same time so I chose to just talk. But to be fair, by secondary school there were no excuses. I was bad at school and I should have just got my head down.'

And at this point Jackiey was trying to persuade her daughter to do just that. She also spent a lot of time trying to get Jade's teachers to be tougher with her and give her more homework so she could catch up. In a bid to give Jade a second chance at education, she was enrolled at Bacon's College in Rotherhithe. Bacon's was one of Britain's first so-called City Technology Colleges, which opened in 1991 as an all-ability school for pupils aged between 11 and 19. 'We have very modern buildings and are well resourced,' says current principal Tony Perry, justifiably proud of his school, its pupils and its achievements.

The college is focused and determined to do the best by

every one of its student intake. But once again Jade fell behind. Still worrying about her mum at home, and unable to spend much time with friends in the evenings, former classmates say Jade was suspended several times and was frequently bullied by other pupils, sometimes fighting back just to survive.

'I used to make Jade go to school with squeezy bottles of lemon to squirt in other girls' eyes,' Jackiey told *Heat* magazine years later, when trying to explain how she tried to protect her vulnerable, surprisingly sensitive daughter. But even at this age Jade's bark seemed to be a lot worse than her bite, and she was gradually developing a strong sense of fair play. 'I even gave her scissors to take to school once, in case she was really bullied,' said her mum. 'But she handed them in.'

Sadly, good behaviour like this has not been remembered and Jade's shadow still seems to loom large over the establishment for the most unfair of reasons. After millions of television viewers had laughed along at the adult Jade's gaffes, mistakes and misunderstandings on *Big Brother*, the college felt the need to put out a statement to say that its exam results have improved greatly since Jade had left. At one point the college apparently felt it might even need to change its name to stop being associated with the shortcomings of its suddenly famous ex-pupil.

And unfortunately Bacon's College wasn't the only local school to feel this way.

Jade's next educational stop had been the Bosco Centre, a registered charity set up in 1984 that accepts pupils between the ages of five and 25. Department head Sister

Cecily Dunn says the centre was specifically set up to 'serve some of the most disadvantaged and disengaged young people in the community, including those who have become disengaged from learning and have challenging behaviour'.

Jade, regrettably, was seen as fitting that description in almost every respect. Educationalists say she was on a cliff edge. A step one way and she would disappear into a chasm of low achievement, probable benefit dependency and possible crime. A step the other way and this could be Jade's last chance to make something of her life.

Thanks to the inspirational Sister Cecily and her team, Jade took a step in the right direction for once. The key aim of the Bosco Centre, according to Sister Cecily, is to give its pupils self-confidence and employability skills so that they can be guided towards full employment and independence. Jade succeeded on all four counts, even though all the odds had always been stacked against her. She was a success, at last.

'Poor old Jade was not very bright, but she came here and tried hard,' says Sister Cecily. 'She got a job and has not done badly at all. My experience is that she is a lovely, warm, friendly girl who is sensitive to other people's feelings.'

But Jade's shadow would still cause temporary problems for other Bosco students in the future. 'People talk of nothing else in relation to Bermondsey but Jade and how thick she is,' Sister Cecily said when *Big Brother* mania was at its height. 'Our young people are very annoyed about it because they feel it suggests that they are stupid when in fact we have very good Ofsted reports and some of our students do go on to university.' Sister Cecily said one pupil had even told her he was planning to take the Bosco Centre's name off his CV because he thought that, post-Jade, it would make employers think he wasn't worth taking on.

Years later, now that Jade has proved she has an extraordinary ability to make the most of her life, it is to be hoped that her former schools are feeling proud rather than ashamed that she was once one of their pupils. Meanwhile, plenty of people don't seem too ashamed to try and find out if they did in fact go to school with Jade and have since forgotten the girl who was so often absent from class. More than two years after *Big Brother* finished, Jade Goody was found to be the sixth most searched-for name on the Friends Reunited website for old school pals. Out of more than seven million searches Jade was also the most looked-for woman on Friends Reunited's list – the five top positions all go to men, with David Beckham at number one, closely followed by Wayne Rooney, Jude Law, Robbie Williams and a certain Mr W Windsor, otherwise known as Prince William.

Not surprisingly, bearing in mind Jade's poor literary skills, she never kept a diary. But from the age of 12 she did put all the key mementos of her life in a shoebox. She calls it her 'secret memory box' and says every young girl should have one. Back then the shoebox came from mid-market store Hobbs – still a stretch for a hard-up teenager from Bermondsey. Since then Jade has carried on collecting – and to reflect her new lifestyle, her secrets now sit in a Gucci shoebox and a Harrod's Easter egg box as well.

'There's nothing of any value in any of them but everything in there means a lot to me,' she says. 'For instance, I have a sachet of sugar from a service station near where my friend and I went skinny-dipping at 15, and tickets from WWF matches from when I was 12.

'The boxes are full of other things, like a badge from the first birthday party I had in McDonald's and autographs I have collected over the years. I've kept love letters too. Of course I haven't had loads, but I've kept the ones that matter. The funniest thing I've kept is a brain scan from when I was seven. I was sent for tests because I was having bad migraines. I asked if I could keep the scan, thinking it would be a picture of my brain but instead it was this long sheet of paper with lines on it. The scan says my brain is normal but other people probably wouldn't agree.

'My most precious thing is the notebook everyone wrote messages in when I left school – like "I will miss your loud mouth". I know I drove teachers mad at school but they got to like me, anyway, so they've written sweet stuff about how they'll always remember me, which is nice.'

That was all the happy stuff. But, as always with Jade, there was sadness too. 'My boxes also hold letters my dad wrote me from prison,' she says, revealing once more how different her childhood was from that of most of her peers. With that always in mind, it is little wonder that Jade always dreamed of escaping and finding a newer, more exciting and less difficult life. Part of the problem was that, back then, Bermondsey itself could feel as if it were playing tricks on its residents.

Geographically speaking, it is right next to the heart of

the capital. From the riverbanks of Rotherhithe, near where Jade was at school, you can stand and look out through Tower Bridge and past the Tower of London to the skyscrapers of the City itself, the legendary Square Mile where fortunes can be made and lost in a day.

But when Jade was a child few rich City brokers had yet decided to make Bermondsey their home. At that time no tube line extended into her troubled manor. Only with the dawn of the new millennium and the extension of the Jubilee Line to Bermondsey, Rotherhithe and Surrey Quays did the yuppies head south-east looking for cheap property and edgy neighbourhoods. Before then, when Jade was a teenager, Bermondsey was always a long bus ride away from the action, so it could feel an insular, sometimes frightening place. The basic rule was that, if you lived there, you stayed there. And Jade was starting to realise that she wanted out. Ironically enough, bearing in mind how her life would turn out, television was her window on to the different world she craved to experience.

'I used to sit at home and watch things like the *Smash Hits Poll Winners' Party* and wish I was there,' she says. And while she daydreamed about the lives and looks of her heroines such as the young Elizabeth Taylor, Jade kept on believing in her father and in the fairy-tale of a perfect family life. It wasn't to come true. 'Dad would say he was coming to see me and never turn up,' she says. The betrayal left deep scars and she says the tense and uncomfortable prison visits she endured as a child were some of the worst days of her life.

Other miseries and doubts were rarely far from the

surface either. Jade was always insecure about her looks – and her figure. And sadly these feelings would be brought back and magnified a hundred times over years later when they were pored over and ridiculed in the newspapers and on television.

'It is hard to believe but when she was younger she was as skinny as a rake,' says market trader granddad John Craddock. 'She had a tiny waist and she used to cry because the other girls had boobs and she didn't. In the end my wife Sylvia bought Jade her first bra and we told her to stuff tissue paper down it so it would look like she had some tits. Now she certainly has them.'

And the teenage Jade was happy to try and make the most of her looks. Her mum had gained far more independence and Jade wanted to catch up with all the partying and good times she had missed. She made good friends in the neighbourhood and started going out to ritzier bars and clubs down the Old Kent Road as well as nearby haunts such as the modern Quebec Curve in Rotherhithe, which serves cocktails alongside pints and family meals. Karaoke nights in local pubs were another favourite for Jade, who loved to be in front of a crowd happily belting out favourites by the likes of everyone from Rod Stewart to Mariah Carey.

At one point Jade and her brother even raised enough money to pay for her to do a course at the prestigious – and expensive – London College of Fashion as a bid to improve her career and social prospects. But Jade admits that at the last minute she decided to spend the cash on a holiday with her friends instead. Escaping from a humdrum life in

Bermondsey looked like it was going to take a lot more willpower, effort and luck.

At 16 Jade lost her virginity to her steady 17-year-old boyfriend – and she remains coy about the subject to this day. 'I know other girls might have done it sooner, but I wanted to wait until it felt right,' she says when pressed. 'We did it in his bedroom. It wasn't all hearts and flowers and rose petals over the bed. But it was nice, comfortable and caring.'

And, as usual, the first person Jade went to afterwards was her mum. 'I had already put myself on the Pill because I am very grown up when it comes to things like that. Mum was pleased for me and was glad I was being careful.'

The pair, who had gone through so much together but were now living full, independent lives, were now far closer than most mothers and daughters. And Jade was always there to support her mum on the one final issue that made the Goody family unique – the fact that Jackiey was gay. 'I'm a lesbian. So what?' Jackiey says bravely today when she is asked about her personal life. But she and Jade both admit it took some time to reach such confidence in this final twist in their extraordinary family tale.

With so many ups and downs in her home life, Jade's employment history was remarkably stable. No one at the Bosco Centre remembers exactly how the idea of Jade becoming a dental nurse had taken hold. But it had seemed a fantastic opportunity for someone who was good with people and was used to caring for others. After passing her initial qualifications and sending out some application forms, she got her first job and life started to improve. Jade found she was good with both patients and staff, and began to thrive.

A more stable future beckoned and as time passed Jade was determined to show that she was getting somewhere, and making something of her life. Unfortunately, in Bermondsey, that meant she needed a bit more than the low salary she was earning at her London dental practice. So she began cutting corners and living beyond her means. As the *Sun* discovered, Jade was £363 in arrears on her council tax by the spring of 2002 and was facing prosecution if she couldn't find the cash fast. But she had so many other demands on her money.

'The right clothes are really important round here, because if you've got them people can see you've made it,' says Jade's Bermondsey neighbour, Shelley McManus. 'Labels are everything: Burberry, Louis Vuitton bags, Donna Karan, Gucci shoes and jewellery from Tiffany's. If it's fake, it has to be good fake.'

'Bermondsey girls know what they want,' agrees another neighbour, Nickola Evans. 'Designer gear and a good night out.'

However, getting that designer gear and living it up in local bars isn't easy when your family has no money, you're earning less than £15,000 a year as a dental nurse and you have debt collectors on your back. So Jade, at 20, was looking for a way out and a way up the social ladder. She was also looking for a way to relieve the growing sense of boredom she was beginning to feel about the relentless nine-to-five world of work.

When she was shown an advert asking for new contestants to move into the *Big Brother* house, she thought she might have found it.

chapter 3

Pick me,
Big Brother!

A friend told Jade about the advert asking for contestants for the new series of Channel 4's Big Brother. The first two shows had been must-see television and had made many of the contestants into overnight stars.

Star-struck Jade had seen pictures of the former housemates in the celebrity magazines and Sunday supplements, all dressed up to the nines at film premières and awards ceremonies. She had watched them do the rounds of chat shows and game shows, and dreamed about the money that they might be making. Even if they were only enjoying that brief 15 minutes of fame, while the clock was ticking they sure seemed to be having fun, she thought. For the celebrity-obsessed 20-year-old in South London, it looked as if your life really could be changed out of all recognition by a television show. And as far as Jade was concerned her life was ready for just such a change.

She was working full-time, but she wasn't earning much. And while her dental practice was based in Covent Garden, one of the liveliest parts of Central London, once inside the surgery her world followed the same basic routine five days a week. In theory being a dental nurse was a good way to meet people – but she pointed out that you can't hold many conversations when your patients are lying back with drills and suction devices in their mouths. And even the good-looking guys lost some of their allure when they were numbed up, in pain and dribbling on their way out of the surgery.

So Jade decided to go for it. If nothing else, *Big Brother* would give her a few weeks away from her day-to-day routine. It would be like a holiday, with all her food and drink paid for by the television company. She would miss her mum and her boyfriend Danny, and she knew that spending her 21st birthday with strangers in the *Big Brother* house, rather than with her friends in a bar in the West End, wasn't a great prospect. But, apart from that, Jade really didn't feel she had much to lose by applying. Because, after all, how bad could it possibly be if she was accepted?

The initial *Big Brother* application form for 2002 was nine pages long and there were two densely typed pages of A4 explaining what was required of potential candidates and why.

As you might imagine, bearing in mind *Big Brother*'s target audience, some of the questions gave the impression that once inside the house almost anything might be possible. 'Are you in a relationship, are you single, or are you a bit of both?' was one of the early queries.

After that the producers asked for some educational and employment details and then got to the personal stuff. 'What might people dislike about you?' 'What is the worst thing you have ever said to anyone, and why?' 'If someone made a film of your life, who would play the lead role?' 'If you could have a famous person (alive or dead) as your mother or father, who would it be and why?'

Mixed within the questions were some interesting requests. 'Write the headline you would least like to see about yourself and the one you would most like to see about yourself if you are in the house,' was the first.

Among her other answers Jade saw former *EastEnders* star Patsy Palmer as the ideal person to play her in a film of her life, and dreamed of having Sean Connery as her father and Sophia Loren as her mother so she would be assured of a glamorous old age. But she certainly didn't guess that 'Ditch the pig!' would have turned out to be one correct answer for her least pleasant headline.

Jade also had to take her time with several of the other questions, which were made particularly tricky by her tortured upbringing and home life. 'Describe your parents,' was one that needed some interesting phrasing. 'Use five words to describe your childhood,' was another.

The next challenge was to produce the two-minute video that the producers wanted to use as a pre-audition tape. Jade's was certainly unique. There were no frills, no fancy camera work and no creative flourishes. Jade just put the camera on a table top at home and stood in front of it wearing tight, light-blue jeans, one of her trademark sparkling wide belts and a tight white T-shirt showing her bare midriff.

First of all she decided she should show the producers her favourite party trick – the fact that she can put her body through an elastic band, which she demonstrated while talking fast, furiously and almost unintelligibly. Straight away the tape was pure Jade Goody.

'I get called Pamela Anderson because of these,' she said, gripping her breasts. 'And Claudia Schiffer when my mates take the piss out of me because I want to be a so-called model.' Little did Jade know at that point that she would soon be called an awful lot worse.

So why should she go on the programme? 'I'd be great for the show because I've got a great personality. I'm very, very bubbly and I'm very outspoken,' she rattled away at the camera. So the producers could hardly say they hadn't been warned. Then came some of the humility and realism for which Jade has been given precious little credit over the years. 'Everyone on *Big Brother* will vote for me, I'm sure of it, not because I'm sure of myself or anything but just because I'm an original,' she said in her typical, convoluted fashion. 'There's not another like me. I'm unique.'

Jade also had a little song to sing – a homage to Rod Stewart, who she idolised. 'Get me out of Bermondsey. And put me on TV. So, Davina and all your friends, pick me,' she sang in a surprisingly decent voice, though without a clearly recognisable tune.

Other audition tapes were far more professional and imaginative than this simple, DIY experiment. But Jade's effort absolutely caught her character. 'The most important thing in the video is to show us who you really are,' say the *Big Brother* producers. Jade's certainly did that. And, while it got her noticed, there was still a long way to go before it got her on the show.

More than 150,000 other people had also sent off for application forms in the early months of 2002, another new record for the show. And the previous year's unexpectedly large total of 5,000 video applications was soon beaten in 2002 as well. At one point the producers in London's Shepherd's Bush were signing in more than 1,000 audition tapes a day and had seen more than 9,150 by the time the closing date arrived.

Nearly three in every four of these applications were dismissed at this stage and the remaining 2,500 hopeful housemates were then called to one of the seven personal audition sites across the country, so the *Big Brother* producers could get a closer look at them. Selectors were after a broad range of characters, ages, backgrounds, races, religions, income groups, jobs and educational standards. They wanted a spark – what TV host Simon Cowell was to call the 'X-factor'. After going through the first batch of applications they thought they might have spotted it in Jade.

So, on 5 March 2002, she headed into London for her live audition. She was nervous on the way to the venue. And she was terrified when she got there. Everyone else seemed older, more worldly, more eloquent and more confident. There were far more men than women there – boys outnumber girls by almost two to one in most *Big Brother* application lists. And many of the women who were there for the auditions were gorgeous, making 20-year-old Jade feel out of her depth from the start. Still, she put the sticky name badge on to her chest and waited in a series of hot, crowded rooms to be called. All around were strangers and rivals. Getting on to *Big Brother* mattered to people. It was certainly starting to matter to Jade.

The first task of the day was to join 24 other hopefuls in a big meeting room. Jade sat on one of the semicircle of chairs set out for them all, took a deep breath and went through all the role-play games, tests and group exercises. One of the biggest challenges was just introducing herself in front of the panel and the other hopeful housemates before the games themselves began. Everyone had to take centre stage in the drab, characterless meeting room and say a few words about themselves – including a secret that would surprise everybody. For someone like Jade, who had no experience of public speaking, it was terrifying. But she did it.

'Just be yourself,' she kept telling herself. 'I'm perfect for this programme. That has to show through.' As the hour-long audition rushed by, Jade found herself holding hands with different applicants in a uniquely complicated game of twister. She had to be ready to ask others a series of questions at random and then answer theirs. It was surprising stuff, according to Jean Ritchie, author of *Inside Big Brother*, with typical questions ranging from the standard 'Are you single?' and 'How long have you had a beard?' to 'What's wrong with the NHS?' and 'Who's your favourite dictator?'

Jade, though terrified, somehow got through it and even

managed to forget that the two *Big Brother* producers were in the room watching and taking notes throughout the morning.

At one point, when Jade's group had been asked to pass a table tennis ball between them all while blindfolded, the two lead producers in the room slipped away to discuss everyone in private. After coming back into the room the producers then congratulated everyone on getting so far and reminded them just how intense competition was that year. Then they announced who they wanted to come back for a more demanding audition later that afternoon. Jade was one of the names they called out.

The next couple of hours were torture. No one would say what the afternoon's tests would involve. And the people who had been called back were told they had to steer clear of each other until their next meetings were called. The whole point of *Big Brother* is that people meet and get to know each other for the first time when they enter the house on live television. Bubble and Brian had met briefly in their auditions the previous year but this had been a complete coincidence. Actual friendships outside the audition rooms are not allowed.

What Jade didn't know was that she had already made a big impression on the producers just to get as far as the afternoon session. 'We're very selective with the under-21s,' said producer Deborah Sargeant, who sat in on many of the London auditions. 'Although in theory we'll take anyone over 18, they have to be especially good to make it through if they are under 21.'

Back in the same meeting room for the second audition,

20-year-old Jade was actually feeling more nervous than she had in the morning – not least because the producers were starting on the infamous 'talk of doom' they constantly repeat to ensure that participants are ready for the *Big Brother* challenge.

'When you come out of the house you will hate the show,' said producer David Williams ominously. 'It will be because everybody has something at the back of their head that they don't really like about themselves, whether it is a physical thing or a personality thing or whatever. You will watch the show and you will see nothing but this flaw magnified a million times. You'll hate it and there will be nothing you can do about it.'

Williams, quoted widely in Channel 4's official *Inside Big Brother* book, had more warnings to give. '*Big Brother* is fundamentally about rejection. You think you have got on well with everybody and made a couple of good friends. Then you find yourself nominated, you find you are the least popular person in the house, and the people you thought were your friends actually dislike you most of all.

'Remember, it is also not just you but your friends and family who will be dragged in. If you are in a relationship, the tabloids may dig around and find someone who will say they have had a passionate affair with you. If you are a parent, you might find yourself dubbed the worst mother or father in Britain for abandoning your children in pursuit of fame and fortune. And the worst thing is, whether it is true or not, you are not there to present your side of the story.'

It was sober stuff. But there was more tough talk to come. The group was given another important warning – they had to keep their audition top secret. The press is always desperate to find out who the next list of *Big Brother* housemates may be. But the producers have one strict rule. If your cover is broken and you are named as a possible contestant, then you are disqualified. End of story.

Silence fell on Jade's group as they digested the warnings and vowed to keep quiet. Then, at least for a while, the fun began again. The producers have a near endless number of games they get their groups to play, so they can see how everyone interacts with each other, who takes the lead, who laughs the loudest, who gets on best with everyone else. Then, suddenly, the mood darkens. The exact arrangements vary for every audition. But at one point in most sessions everyone is handed a pen and paper, and told to write down the name of the person they want to leave the audition and be sent home. Writing down a reason is optional.

The producers then add up the names, announce the result and tell the loser to leave the room – but only as far as into the next room, where they will be the first to be interviewed in front of a video camera. The eviction threat wasn't real, the relief in the group is palpable and everyone has learned another important *Big Brother* lesson. 'People have all just experienced the complex pain of rejection, either by feeling it when their names were read out or by inflicting it,' says *Inside Big Brother* author Jean Ritchie.

Jade laughed nervously when her turn came to sit in

front of the camera in the interview room and she laughed again and again as she tried to answer all the producer's questions. She was both nervous and natural, they said when discussing her later. And both attributes were attractive to them.

Heading back to Bermondsey that night with the far larger follow-up questionnaire in her bag, Jade had no idea how well she had performed. A tiny part of her was optimistic because she had never imagined she would get this far, and because being asked to take part in the one-on-one recorded interview seemed to suggest they were serious about her. What she didn't know was that nearly 650 other individual interviews were being taped around the country. The competition was as tough as ever.

Within a week this vast number of applicants had been narrowed down to just 120 desperate housemates and in late March nearly three dozen people in the *Big Brother* family – which included even the lowliest 'runners' who ran errands for the main producers – sat in a meeting room for almost 12 hours. They watched the audition tapes and recorded interviews of each candidate, reviewed their application forms, read the reports written on all of them and put one in every three in the 'reject' pile.

Jade's file survived. So she got a mysterious call asking her to stand alone outside a fast-food outlet in a quiet London street the next day. She would be met, she was told, by a *Big Brother* staffer. The cloak-and-dagger operation has one key purpose, according to the production staff. Someone from the production team keeps a watch on the potential housemate long before the agreed meeting time, to check that they haven't brought a photographer or anyone else along with them, because the producers' biggest fear is inadvertently selecting a journalist for the show. When Jade was seen to be alone, her minder for the day approached and, in a military-style operation, got her into the interview location without accidentally seeing any of the other potential housemates who were being chaperoned on neighbouring streets.

Her final day of interviews was gruelling and Jade finally met the top three people in the *Big Brother* hierarchy. She spent an hour in a room with executive producer Phil Edgar-Jones and series editors Helen Hawkin and Gigi Eligoloff. Any one of this top trio could have ended Jade's *Big Brother* adventure with a single word. But they didn't – they liked her. So Jade was sent one more step down the line for another long meeting with the show's full-time psychotherapist Brett Kahr. Brett's role in *Big Brother* is shrouded in secrecy – unlike many of the other mental-health experts employed by the producers he never appears on screen. But he is available 24 hours a day for private chats in the Diary Room once housemates are in the show. And before then he is given complete power of veto over who is selected for the programme. If Phil, Helen and Gigi were all set on one particular applicant and Brett says he doesn't think that they have the right stuff for the challenge, then they're off the list. It's that simple.

Luckily, Jade passed Brett's mental tests with flying colours. But still the selection process went on. *Big Brother* producer Endemol has to check the medical and police records of potential housemates. It says that, while the information on them may not rule people out of contention, it has to be known about in advance, in case there are complications later. 'Having a police record won't necessarily exclude you from the show,' says one producer. 'But lying about it will.'

Once more Jade Goody made it through to the next stage. She was then told exactly when the show would be filmed, so she could ensure she was available for the whole nine-week show, plus at least one week afterwards if she won. She sat through the first professional photo shoots of her life – something she loved and would soon be doing a whole lot more of. She was called back for another talk of doom by the producers and another long interview with Brett. Then, as one of the final 24 in the participant pool, Jade was asked to sign a contract to the show and make a legal declaration that everything she had told them so far was true, and that she would keep everything that had happened so far confidential. She was getting more nervous by the day, and finding it harder than ever to carry on with her normal routines without telling everyone what was going on and risking the whole operation.

Meanwhile, more fierce arguments were going on in the *Big Brother* headquarters as the 24 hopefuls were finally taken down to the final 12 who would actually go into the house. Jade nearly fainted when she was told the news by the show's top man, Phil Edgar-Jones. 'I thought Jade was going to collapse when I rang her, she was hyperventilating.

I had to tell her to sit down and take a few deep breaths,' he said.

Hardly able to believe it, Jade started to panic again as soon as she had put the phone down. It was all coming true. She was actually going to be on national television in the *Big Brother* house – and she had better get ready because it was all due to begin in less than 10 days' time.

chapter 4

In the House

After two nights in a secret hotel in Central London with her Big Brother minder, Jade was finally on her way to the house itself. A fleet of identical, silver-grey chauffeur-driven cars had been hired to drive each housemate to the fortress-like Big Brother compound in Elstree, Hertfordshire, and Jade peered out of the windows in shock as she saw how many people had gathered there to watch the show.

This, the third series of *Big Brother*, had been massively promoted in the media for nearly a month and anticipation levels were high. The tabloids had been full of conjecture about what sort of housemates and challenges the show's producers had up their sleeves to spice things up in 2002. '*Big Brother* is getting tough,' was one of the show's key slogans. And the prospective housemates were getting nervous.

More than a thousand people had turned up to watch

the housemates go into the compound and they lined the road cheering wildly as the cars slowed and approached their final destinations: the start of the 'walk of fame' that would end with Davina McCall and the door to what was temporarily the most famous house in Britain.

That night Jade was wearing an off-the-shoulder tight black top with one billowing sleeve, a sparkling silver belt and tight black trousers. She had wanted to look cool and a little bit funky but hadn't wanted to dress stupidly just to grab attention. Looking at herself in the mirror with her mum before leaving the hotel room, she hoped she had pitched it just about right.

'Wave, smile and enjoy it. It's your first big moment in the spotlight so have fun. You may never get this kind of positive reaction again,' *Big Brother* housemates are told before they head for the house on the first day of the show. Jade was determined to lap up all the attention, though she was shaking and terrified as she prepared to get out of the car and face the public. Once she was on her way, her female minder walked a couple of paces behind to provide moral as well as physical support as the crowds roared and cheered and tried to reach out and touch Jade over the barriers.

The *Big Brother* theme tune was blaring out through the massive speakers as Davina grabbed each housemate for some final words – giving the public at home a first chance to size up the people they would be following for the rest of the summer.

Brief interview and final hugs with family and friends over, Jade then climbed up the shiny metal staircases, across the suspended platforms, through the final gates to the door to the house itself. There, in front of the huge crowds and on live television, she was frisked for a final time and told to walk through the silver doors into the *Big Brother* house. She would stay there for the next nine, long weeks.

'I can manage, I can manage,' were her first words inside the house as she tried to get her suitcase down the staircase herself before Sandy rushed up to help her. Jade was the third girl, and the ninth out of the 12 housemates to enter the house, and the people she met were a mixed bunch. There was kilt-wearing Sandy, who at 43 was older than Jade's father, the gorgeous male model Alex, the ebullient Brummie Alison, the shaven-headed PJ – and before Jade could say her hellos and greet the others, the final housemates started coming down the stairs to add to the confusion.

One of the late arrivals turned out to be a friendly face Jade thought she recognised from the London auditions – trainee barrister Kate Lawler. The pair greeted each other with a shriek and then clung to each other for support in those first few moments. But, as everyone would see, they would never really become friends.

That year's house, and the *Big Brother* compound itself, had been created by set designer Markus Blee, the man behind the sets for *TFI Friday* and *The Priory*. Built directly on top of the concrete reservoir that had served as a set for the 1955 film *The Dam Busters*, the *Big Brother* compound was bigger than before, with two communal bedrooms that had a mixture of single and double beds, an open-plan kitchen and lounge area. Outside there was decking for sunbathing, a grass area, a huge Jacuzzi, and the soon-to-be-famous chicken coop. Inside, the overall feel was of a trendy, city slicker's bachelor pad. And you would hardly know that it was also the centre of a massive media operation.

The largely prefabricated building had cost around £450,000 to build and had taken 75 workmen nearly 20 weeks to complete. Just under 20 km of cable connected 250 studio-strength lights, 50 microphones, 28 fixed surveillance cameras and five manned cameras.

Behind the 50 one-way observation mirrors around the compound there was also a small army of intense *Big Brother* workers. The show's production team was more than 300-strong, with shifts on duty 24 hours a day. Staff watched the live camera feeds on 50 screens in the main control room. They edited the coverage down for the nightly shows, looked in on the housemates, waited to speak to them through the compound-wide sound system and controlled absolutely everything and everyone.

And nothing was left unobserved or unrecorded. More than 5,000 long-play videotapes of footage would build up in the production offices over the course of the show and the public was able to watch on Channel 4, on the digital channel E4 and on the Internet. There were live shows every day, plus the evening highlights and big eviction specials. It was going to be saturation stuff.

'Before we all have to start kicking each other out, as nasty as it is, this is to us,' said fireman Jonny, proposing a toast to the whole group on their first evening. 'No matter

what happens, let's have a good laugh and keep in touch.'
On reflection, it seems he was being staggeringly optimistic.

'This house, this atmosphere. Everything is going to
change in a couple of weeks,' said fitness instructor Lee.
He couldn't have been more right, because this was going
to be the most contentious and argument-filled show to
date. At one point, if many of the housemates kept it
touch, it looked as if it would have to be done through
their solicitors.

Still, the first few days of incarceration were fantastic –
for Jade and for almost everyone else. The group did
congas in the hot tub; there was plenty of food and drink,
plenty of places to lounge around and talk – and plenty to
talk about. Everyone was nervous, but everyone was
smiling. For about 24 hours.

The first of the show's big arguments came as early as
Day 2. And, starting as she meant to go on, Jade was right
in the middle of it. The whole group was sitting around the
square of orange sofas talking about drugs and addiction.
After things got increasingly heated, trainee barrister
Sunita lost patience with Jade and told her off for
interrupting and not following her argument. 'You're too
young and you don't listen,' said the 25-year-old. 'You
don't understand the nature of addiction, you're too naïve.'

Jade, rarely credited for restraint or for keeping silent,
knew she could have gone for the sympathy vote and won
some friends and some credibility at this point. But she
chose not to. She restrained herself.

'I never mentioned all that in the house because I'm not
that sort of person. I didn't want to drag everyone down

with me. I'm a happy person and my childhood didn't matter. Being in the house was just about enjoying myself and living in the moment,' she said when the row with Sunita was discussed after the show had ended.

Sunita, regrettably, didn't know about Jade's troubled family history. So their row got more intense than it should have done. And it was to be the first of many.

On Day 3, Jade was the first person to cry in the house – tears born of a mixture of homesickness, nerves and intimidation. Apart from Jade, the average age of the contestants was nearly 27. She was just 20 – the youngest person to have been in the programme so far. And it was already beginning to show. For a start, she was terrified of missing out on anything, and was worried about offending anyone by leaving any conversation or gathering too soon.

So the girl known as 'Baby Brother' and 'Big Brother's baby' stayed up late every night, gossiping, drinking and laughing nervously. She was desperate to impress, trying to please and hoping to win friends in this older, more worldly group. At the back of her mind, Jade, alongside all the other housemates, was also aware that the public's opinion of them all mattered. As far as they knew they would have a week or 10 days to settle down before they would be required to nominate which two of the 12 housemates would then go up for the show's first public vote. But the producers had other ideas. And the show's eviction schedule was further thrown into disarray by the unexpected and voluntary departure of two of the housemates.

The first of the 12 to walk was Sunita, who said that she could no longer cope with the atmosphere and the challenges in the house. She asked to leave early and, on Day 7, was led away through the compound's secret back door. These unexpected events meant that the first real eviction of the series took place on Day 8 after one week in the house. And it was sprung on the housemates like a bolt from the blue.

'Housemates, this is Davina. You are live on Channel 4. Please do not swear.' Davina's voice rang out over the compound's loudspeakers to tell the housemates to gather in the living room – where they were all in for a shock. 'When we closed the doors on you last Friday we opened the voting to the public,' Davina explained. 'All week they have been nominating the housemates they would like to leave the *Big Brother* house. The two housemates with the most nominations are up for eviction. The first eviction is happening tonight.'

And there was more drama to come. The two players the public liked least turned out to be Jade and 36-year-old Lynne. They were banished to the boy's bedroom because *Big Brother* had another evil idea to explain: the remaining housemates had to make the final decision of who would stay and who would walk. It was the exact opposite of all the previous evictions, where housemates made the initial choice and left the final twist of the knife to the public. In 2002 *Big Brother* had clearly decided to make things more personal and potentially trigger more divisions within the group.

'Lynne and Jade, you have been nominated by the public,' said Davina over the sound system, which piped into every corner of the house. 'The rest of you now have three minutes to decide who to evict. How you decide is up to you. Your three minutes start now.'

The girls clung to each other on the bed waiting to hear the verdict of their peers. And, after what seemed like an eternity, it came. The housemates had voted to evict Lynne.

'It's horrible, it's all wrong,' Jade cried in the bedroom, hugging Lynne tightly and trying to comfort her after Davina had announced the news. But the fact that Jade had survived the eviction threat ultimately seemed to matter less to her than the manner in which she had survived it. She got a huge confidence boost when she found out that the other housemates had voted unanimously in her favour. Every one of them had wanted Jade to stay in the gang, not sent back to the outside world. 'Jade's like my baby sister. She's full of love and we've all taken her under our wing,' said the usually gruff Jonny, trying to explain their actions to Lynne while she tearfully packed her bag to leave.

Once the Scottish student had left the house, Jade was finally able to say how worried she had been about leaving. 'I just wanted my mummy to cuddle,' she said when the housemates asked her what it felt like to hear her name put up for eviction. She had been desperately keen to make sure her *Big Brother* adventure didn't end so early. As a long-term fan of the show and an avid reader of celebrity magazines, she knew that the people who left the house in the first few weeks were the soonest forgotten and the least likely to get invited to more than a few C-list events.

Jade was dreaming of much more than that and she certainly wasn't ready to face such a public rejection. Finding out that the people she had spent 24 hours a day with disliked her enough to vote her out would have been a devastating blow to someone like Jade. All the noise, the jokes and the shouting hid Jade's vulnerabilities and insecurities. She had spent her life wanting to be loved. Eviction would be crystal-clear evidence that she wasn't.

Sadly, if the public had been given the final say, her eviction would have been certain. As early as the first week of the show she wasn't just bottom of the official online poll for the most popular housemates – she was bottom by a mile. Meanwhile, the media had begun its massive hate campaign against the Bermondsey girl, with commentators and columnists lining up to tell readers to vote her out. Graham Norton, of whom more later in this book, had begun his attacks on her in his nightly show. 'They had 150,000 applicants and in the final equation – Jade. How did that happen? God, she's annoying. If it wasn't cruel to kick a pig, you would,' was one of his kinder comments. Elsewhere, such was the strength and ferocity of the anti-Jade campaign that Ladbrokes and other bookies stopped taking on new bets about her eviction after the first few days of the show.

But survive she did. And for a few weeks, at least, she was going to thrive. Jade's temporary happy patch began on Day 13 – her 21st birthday. After dreaming that no one in the house wanted to celebrate it with her, and being too afraid to come out of the bedroom in case it was true, she ended up having a fantastic day. She might not be spending it with her oldest friends, as she had always imagined, but she was spending it with new friends and that felt pretty good as well.

Outside the bedroom the housemates were ready with presents – including a bracelet from PJ. Meanwhile, Kate had baked her some birthday biscuits, and Alex and Sophie were vying to cook her a birthday breakfast. Relieved and excited, Jade headed back to the bedroom to dress up for her big day. And to find that *Big Brother* had a tough choice for her.

In the Diary Room she was given the option of seeing a video message from her mother or a back-to-school party for the rest of the housemates. Jade made her decision fast, but it preyed on her mind for the rest of the day so she kept going over and over it, to justify it to herself and to everyone else. 'I'd love to see the message from my mum. But I'm sorry, Mum, I'll see you when I get out. I'd like to have a party, please,' she told *Big Brother* in the Diary Room. 'I see my mum every day but I'm never going to get to celebrate my birthday in here again,' she told the others afterwards, worrying if she had done the wrong thing. And later still she cried out, 'Mum, I love you to bits, but sorry, this is my birthday,' when the drink had begun to flow.

And flow it did. The party was fancy dress with everyone in school uniforms ready to help blow out the candles on Jade's cake (she didn't need any assistance, strangely enough) and start a nine-and-a-half-hour drinking binge. 'I'm going to get so lagging – cheers, my dears,' said Jade, toasting her housemates with wine as the celebrations began. And part of the reason for the great evening was the fact that the housemates got to enjoy a rare luxury in honour of Jade's big day – music. Evictees say one thing they found hardest to get used to in the *Big Brother* environment was the lack of noise. There is no television, no radio and no CDs in the house in a bid to force the housemates to talk and to interact far more than they would in everyday life. It meant that the single hour of disco music Jade had been allocated as her birthday treat triggered some real highs and some surprising bonding.

Outside the house, viewers had been asked to vote on which song would close Jade's old school disco. They picked George Michael's 'Careless Whisper' – one of her long-time favourites along with Mariah Carey's 'Heart Breaker'. And when the song was over the partying went on until Jade and everyone else finally ran out of steam and got ready to suffer some of the biggest hangovers of the series.

The way Jade threw herself wholeheartedly into enjoying her birthday seemed to have had an effect on the public. The day before, she had been just one place from last on the online popularity poll – her highest position so far. But within a week she would be the most popular housemate in the show. And, barring a few hiccups, she would stay near the top of the chart almost every day till the very end of the nine-week run.

But in Week 2 Jade and all the other housemates were to face some unexpected new competition in the popularity stakes. The first surprise came two days after Sunita's departure – the arrival of beautiful recruitment consultant Sophie, whose rows with Jade were to become the talk of the house, and the country. But before then it was time for someone else to be evicted. Alex, Alison and Sandy were nominated at the end of Week 2 – and Alison turned out to be the second evictee, and the third to leave the *Big Brother* house.

The remaining housemates didn't have much time to relax when she had left because there was yet another big surprise round the corner. While the housemates were locked away in the bedrooms, the living quarters were being divided into two by a line of clear plastic bars. Housemates were told that one side would be the 'rich' half of the compound, where housemates could live in luxury with great food, home comforts and regular treats. The other would be the 'poor' side, where housemates had to suffer an outside toilet, cold showers and would end up arguing over whether a spoonful of sugar in a coffee was a waste of precious, communal resources.

True to her life so far, Jade was allocated a space on the poor side of the world. It felt like the council house in Bermondsey all over again. Die-hard *Big Brother* fans still say the house divide was a mistake. They say that, while it did magnify some tensions, it also killed the vital interaction between all of the housemates and it has never been repeated in any subsequent show. But, for all the downsides, it did raise some passions – and helped push personal shopper Sandy over the edge.

The 43-year-old was slowly going stir-crazy in the house, failing to bond with many of his fellow competitors, and frequently clashing with Jade. And pretty soon he had had enough. On Day 19 he announced that he was planning to leave the next morning. And, after famously relieving himself in the kitchen bin when everyone else was sleeping, he climbed up the wall and over the house roof to freedom.

Sandy too was soon replaced – by handsome rich kid Tim. To be fair, the 23-year-old graduate wasn't the happiest of housemates. But with the single word 'comprendez' he at least ensured that not every *Big Brother* catchphrase would be coined by Jade that year.

And just after Lee lost out to Jonny and became the latest evictee, Jade was going to coin another one: 'minging'. Years later Jade is remembered for many, many things in the *Big Brother* house. This one would begin with something very, very small: a verruca on her foot. Jade first spotted it while having a shower on the morning of Day 26. And she wasn't pleased.

She stormed into the main living area, where most of the other housemates were having a quiet breakfast. 'What's the matter, baba?' Jonny asked using the nickname he had created for her in the show's first few days. Jade was almost too incoherent and too upset to explain. But it clearly involved her favourite word.

'I have discovered a verruca on my finger and on my toe from this minging house,' was how it began.

'But you can't get a verruca on your finger,' Kate said, to no avail.

'Minging!' Jade screamed. 'This minging shower. It's disgusting. My toe is minging. I've never had anything like that. This minging, dirty *BB* house!'

Screaming at the world in general over this indignity wasn't enough for Jade. She had to bring others into the row – and she did so by focusing on a comment, and a look, that she had received from former best pal Adele. Jade mistakenly thought the 23-year-old had given her a dirty look and had insulted her. She didn't take it well.

Her anger in the bedroom was awesome, unrestrained and grotesque. She refused to listen to Adele's explanations or accept her apologies. She screamed at and over her – lashing out at hopeful peacemaker Alex in the process. If she was lost for words for even a few seconds, she was soon back with another accusation, another repetition of why and how she had been so unfairly attacked. It was fantastic, riveting television that would be repeated endlessly in the coming weeks.

While at the time it seemed as if Jade's anger would never stop, she did suddenly collapse. Viewers saw her sitting on the bed, crying in Alex's arms quite literally like a baby. Her whole face was crumpled and tear-stained, her nose bright red and her eyes scared. It was like absolutely nothing else on television that summer – and ratings soared as the show became the most talked-about event of the year.

What audiences then saw was that Jade could forgive and forget as quickly as she could flare up in a rage. She and Adele were soon hugging and apologising, and talking once more about possibly sharing a flat together when the show was over. As it turned out, that was never going to happen, and there were more storms to come between the girls. Meanwhile, someone else was to prove to have an even more intense, volatile and intimate love–hate relationship with Jade. It was PJ.

He and Jade had been flirting pretty much from the start. 'I'm not going to show you my boobs. Behave,' she said one night in the bedroom, not really aware just how well they could be seen and heard through *Big Brother*'s high-tech night-vision cameras and omnipresent microphones.

But the flirting would continue, and after nearly three weeks of pretend passion things suddenly got a whole lot more exciting. As Channel 4's brilliant Geordie continuity announcer Marcus Bentley said, 'One night, after 10 hours of drinking, PJ and Jade had a night they couldn't remember but the rest of us couldn't forget.'

Dubbed by Davina McCall as 'the fumble in the jungle', it was the night that the long-running 'Will anyone, won't anyone?' debate about sex in the *Big Brother* house finally seemed to get a positive answer. The hazy night-sight images showed Jade getting into the next bed to PJ. She had taken off her T-shirt and it was hard to tell if he was still wearing his boxers. The pair whispered and giggled. Then Jade sneaked out of her bed and slipped under the law student's sheets. There were more mutterings, more giggles and more movement.

Commentators said video freeze-frames hadn't been used so much since Sharon Stone's infamous crossing-the-legs scene in *Basic Instinct*. Viewers across the country – including 'outraged' newspaper editors desperate to sell more papers – were trying to work out exactly what body part was where and who was who under PJ's duvet. Despite the fuzzy images, the consensus was that the couple had done more than just hold hands. It had been 'PJ's BJ' as one paper called it and 'Jade had gone down in television history', according to another.

But it wasn't going to be the start of any great romance. Jade stayed in bed until very late the morning after the night before. 'Did I snog you last night?' a bashful PJ whispered across at her.

'No, you never. You must have dreamed it,' she replied.

But PJ wasn't ready to let it rest until Jade started to get annoyed. 'Look, I'm not bothered. You're making more of a scene about it than me. Stop making a big deal about it,' she said.

So PJ headed into the living-room area to face the others – and effectively turned the knife into his former bedfellow. He gave some pretty explicit gestures to suggest what they had been up to under the sheets. But then tried to suggest that Jade had done all the running. 'I don't even fancy her,' he whispered, after looking around to check that she was still in the bedroom.

Later that day, viewers got the chance to squirm with pity as Jade hugged her man at the barbeque the team had been preparing for lunch. He held back, however, keeping his hands firmly in his pockets and refusing to make eye contact or even lean towards her. It was a painful scene – subsequently voted one of the most memorable of the series – and Jade then headed back inside. She was a quiet and suddenly lonely figure, pulling the glass door closed behind her and giving one final, sad look towards PJ. It was hard not to feel sorry for her, and she was rewarded by another strong position in that week's online popularity poll.

While all these must-watch arguments and incidents were going on, two more housemates had been evicted. Spencer was ousted at the end of Week 4, Sophie at the end of Week 5. But it was at the end of Week 6 that the housemates would get a rude awakening and a horrible reminder of the outside world.

Adele's name was called out by Davina on the usual Friday-night eviction show. The fit and fun DJ from Southport went through all the usual routines. There were hugs, kisses, tearful goodbyes. She headed up the 18 steps to the house doors, waited for the instruction to leave and then stepped forward to face the outside world. Then she stopped. The 23-year-old was being booed by the crowd. But the door to the house was closing behind her. She had nowhere to hide, and had to run into the gauntlet.

Back inside, the remaining housemates stood in shock. Previously they had only heard the crowd cheering on eviction nights. And if someone as fundamentally decent as Adele could get treatment like this, what lay in store for them? Just what was going on out there? 'Bloody hell,' said Alex, as everyone looked at each other in horror. 'Why the hell was *she* being booed?'

'It must have been like somebody dropping a breeze block on your head,' said Jonny later, when they all relived how Adele had frozen, temporarily, as the jeers had rung out.

That night everyone in the house realised the enormity of what they were part of. They didn't know how many people might be watching them 24 hours a day on television and on the Internet. But they could tell that huge numbers were outside the house every eviction night. And they now knew that passions were high and that the crowd's judgements were harsh.

And Jade soon realised that she was being judged the most harshly. This fun, relaxing game show was suddenly getting serious. The tone had changed. 'Something, something, you fat something,' she said in shock, trying to piece together some new shouting which was clearly about her. 'Oh my God, everyone outside hates me. I might be the most hated person in London.' Surprisingly quiet, she mulled over her prospects. They didn't look good. 'I don't want to go out there and for everyone to be horrible,' she said almost to herself, preparing for the worst. Suddenly, going on national television didn't seem to have been such a good way to change or improve her life after all. Had she made a massive mistake and ruined everything?

Under siege and scared, Jade found she wasn't going to get much sympathy or support from the other equally worried housemates. Once again she was on her own with her fears, and as her nerves got out of control she started acting even more recklessly. And this led almost directly to the infamous evening when Jade was persuaded to take her clothes off.

chapter 5

Acting like a Chipstick

It was Day 47 and the vast Big Brother production team had started to relax. The show was way ahead of last year's in the ratings, taking Channel 4's nightly share of the television audience to near record levels. They were making big money in phone and text votes and through the new Internet viewing services. And they had made more than enough newspaper headlines out of the likes of Jade to keep even the keenest publicist happy.

Far from looking tired and outdated, the *Big Brother* franchise looked healthier than ever. And that was no mean achievement in World Cup summer, when the country had gone football crazy and every other channel was under pressure to find audiences for non-sporting shows. Tantrums, tears, walkouts, screaming matches, sexual chemistry and even the hint of sex itself: this series of *Big Brother* had already had it all. When it came to becoming a national talking point, could things get any better? It turned out that they could, because, in terms of making the news, Jade was about to move up a gear. Once again she was going to be centre stage when she created one of the defining moments of the whole *Big Brother* phenomenon.

It all began with the housemates relaxing on the sofas in the living room playing a word-association game and drinking heavily. Not surprisingly, bearing in mind her slow verbal skills, Jade was losing. And, to make matters worse, the boys had decided that, every time you lost a question, you had to take off another item of clothing.

Analysis of the videotapes afterwards suggests they were also rigging the questions to ensure that Jade always got the tough ones. Game for a laugh, and worried about getting a reputation as a bad loser that could inflame the jeering crowds outside still further, Jade did what she was told. She took off her T-shirt and jeans when she lost in the first few rounds. And then off came her bra. And then there was very little left.

'I can't take my knickers off,' she screeched when she lost yet again and was almost completely naked.

'We all agreed so you'd better do it,' countered the laughing figures around her on the sofas.

So, of course, Jade went ahead, slowly pulling her last remaining piece of clothing down her legs and sitting curled up into a ball of embarrassment on the living-room sofa.

To compound her awful vulnerability, everyone else in the room was fully clothed. Just across the coffee table, PJ was unable to look at her. Alex, in the kitchen, fell on to the floor in shock. Jonny and Tim nearly fell off their own chairs as they recoiled from the spectacle in front of them. Even Kate, the one other woman left in the house, was aghast, too stunned to summon up any female solidarity or perhaps throw Jade a towel so she could cover up.

Marooned on the sofa, cameras whirring overhead, knowing that her mum, friends, employers and millions of strangers were no doubt watching at home, Jade did the only thing she could think of. She stood up. Then she ran desperately out of the room and into the *Big Brother* history books.

Channel 4 says a near record of 5.8 million people were watching when the full monty happened – and the computer press reported that Internet systems were overloaded over the next few days as people across the country e-mailed each other a series of still and moving pictures of the action.

Two years later, that scene was to be voted the best from all five series of the show. And it wasn't the only one in the top 10 that featured Jade. When the official *Big Brother Uncut 3* highlights video and DVD were released after the show, the box listed just three key events to attract buyers. Two of them involved Jade, and series winner Kate didn't even merit a mention.

What the *Big Brother Uncut 3* highlights did focus on, however, was the bitching and gossiping that dominated the series. And back inside the house, as Week 7 got under way, Jade was once more to be under fire for allegedly leading the bad behaviour. 'All you do now is argue,' said PJ in one of the big row's over Jade's character. She was being called 'childish', 'a two-faced bitch', 'a back-stabber' and worse. But was all this fair?

'There was a real tendency for frustrations to be vented disproportionately on Jade,' said psychologist Dr Sandra Scott from London's Maudsley Hospital.

'It was a classic case of mobbing,' said the show's in-house psychologist Peter Collett.

Meanwhile, others said that clever editing was being used to portray Jade – and the others – in ways that would make them most interesting to viewers. So a hero or heroine one day could be made to look like the exact opposite the next. And if Jade was guilty of serial bitching then it is only fair to say that she was certainly not alone.

'In this series bitching reached epidemic proportions, with several types of bitching being employed, not all of them immediately obvious,' said Peter Collett, after reviewing the tapes and working out exactly who was doing what and how. And first of all Jade did indeed seem to have been identified as the worst of the group. 'Jade often engages in open bitching, where she addresses several people simultaneously,' said Collett. But was this as bad as it sounded? As Jade herself would say, in many respects this is actually the most honest type of gossip because she was not hiding in a corner trying to avoid answering for her opinions. Collett, ultimately, would agree with her – though Jade struggled to get the message across to her housemates.

'You've probably talked about everyone that's in this house behind their back,' accused PJ during one typical row.

'Yes, I have. But I've gone up to them and told them,' she

fought back, determined to prove that she had guts and integrity. 'You can trust me to the ground because, if I think something, I say it.'

Nick Chambers, editor of *TV Hits* magazine, was also ready to bring some perspective to the back-stabbing debate and to give Jade the benefit of the doubt over the bitching claims. 'Her tendency to talk about people behind their backs may have been exaggerated or misunderstood,' he said. 'It may look like bitching to us but maybe it is no worse than what we all do every day.' And it is impossible to deny that the deliberate tensions of having people live in such close proximity, for so long, and with no outside influences or distractions, clearly tainted the relationships between the housemates.

'If we met on the outside, we'd get on,' Kate told Jade in the final week as they made up after yet another massive row. But they hadn't met that way. And in this pressure-cooker environment the pair would never really be able to put their bad feelings behind them. Of the other housemates, PJ at least tried to bury the hatchet with Jade before he was evicted from the house at the end of Week 7. 'Sorry about last week. A bit awkward,' was his final mumble to her as he headed up the stairs, out of her life and back into reality.

With PJ gone, there were just five housemates left. Jade, Kate, Alex, Jonny and late arrival Tim. Tension was mounting but Jade was determined to try and ease it. On her audition tape and application form, she had said she thought she would be good fun to have in the house. As the nine-week incarceration drew towards its close, she also turned out to be a pretty good sport – still prepared to play the fool and laugh at herself if it would help to lift the group's mood on low days. She was also prepared to accept more than her fair share of mildly cruel insults.

She laughed it off when she was constantly compared to Pat Butcher from *EastEnders*, for example – though it is hard to imagine that many 21-year-olds would be happy to be told they reminded people of a sixty-something actress, whose character is famed for her hard living and rough looks. No one was prepared to say Jade scrubbed up well either. When Kate helped her with her make-up, the normally supportive Jonny told her she looked like a drag queen.

When she burned herself making popcorn one evening and realised she now had three scars on her hand, she didn't get much support either. 'Who's gonna marry me now with a scabby hand? And a potbelly? And a fat ass? And big lips? And double chin?' she asked plaintively.

'And that silly voice? Nobody,' said Jonny dismissively.

Even that wasn't the final insult to a girl who had said in her audition tape that she thought she looked a bit like Pamela Anderson. Alex said he disagreed. He thought Jade looked like Thora Hird, who at the time was 90.

But still Jade was determined to keep on entertaining the others. 'Bark like a dog,' Alex shouted at her when she was trying to show off some exercise moves. She gave it a go.

'Do cartwheels, Jade,' followed up Tim. And again Jade was up for the challenge even if the housemates didn't always appreciate her efforts.

'I'm feeling lower than a cockroach's legs,' she had said

quietly on Day 59 after her big party piece – dressing up as a spaceman to entertain the others with a Babylon Zoo song – fell flat and failed to raise many laughs. 'I think I speak for everyone when I say that was s**t,' said Alex.

Just as eye-catching were Jade's bizarre beauty regimes. The face masks and cucumbers on the eyes with Kate. Squeezing her spots in the one-way mirrors – then dabbing toothpaste on her face in the hope that this would make the mess go away.

Pulling a rubber band round her body had been her party trick on the *Big Brother* application video. In the house her headline act was to put her whole fist into her mouth – an image which would, unknown to her, dominate the next day's newspapers.

'I've got a massive gob with big lips as well,' she said, surprisingly proudly. 'I can fit a four-finger KitKat in that way as well. Sideways.' And there were times when her housemates and viewers would have happily provided Jade with a box full of KitKats so she could perform the trick. Just to try and shut her up. Her ability to talk became legendary from Day 1, not least because she would happily chatter on, even when she had nothing much to say. PJ called her 'the mad one' and she happily admitted that she had got 'the biggest trap in the house'.

Unknown to her, Jade also talked in her sleep, which is embarrassing enough at the best of times, but is made a hundred times worse when you are being filmed 24 hours a day and your bedroom is rigged up with the latest night-vision cameras and always-on microphones.

With just five housemates left and the dividing bars long

gone, the *Big Brother* compound started to feel far bigger. The residents could easily divide up into smaller splinter groups and huddle in corners for private discussions. It was Jade's worst nightmare, because she couldn't bear to be left out of anything and was always terrified that she was the subject of everyone else's gossip. The relaxed mood she had tried to share with the rest of the group since the two sides of the house had been reunited suddenly disappeared. No longer prepared to play the fool, Jade became more tense, her behaviour increasingly irrational.

Viewers knew this meant only one thing: yet another Jade Goody eruption was on the cards. It was going to be a big one. And we didn't have to wait very long to see it.

The final build-up came during the alcohol-fuelled '70s disco party on Day 55. At first everything looked great. One of the bedrooms had been kitted out with everything from beanbags to a disco ball. Everyone had fantastic, over-the-top, retro costumes and devised individual personas to suit them. Alex, in a huge Afro wig, was Leroy Love. Tim, loving his yellow nylon kit, was Sven the Swedish Porn Director. Cat-suited Kate was Lucy Love Lips, and Jonny was Lionel Vinyl.

Jade, who was dubbed Horny Helga, put on some blue eyeshadow and a blonde wig, and said she was aiming to look like Abba babe Agnetha. Not everyone agreed. 'You look like one of those woman wrestlers,' said Tim crushingly.

At this point even this sort of comment couldn't hit the group's mood. They sang some Abba and Bee Gees songs unaccompanied while they waited for the real music to be piped in to them. They started eating the prawn cocktails and other '70s-style food. And, of course, they started drinking.

The booze led to some pretty raunchy dirty dancing – and then Kate and Jonny started to worry Jade by talking and whispering together throughout the evening. Jade and Alex then started talking in the bedroom – with Alex winding up the 21-year-old about whether or not Kate and Jonny had been talking about her behind her back. Suddenly convinced that Alex was right, Jade headed off to confront the pair and got even more suspicious and angry to discover they were locked away together in the Diary Room. For 45 minutes.

When they finally came out, Jade's attack was ferocious. 'Quite clearly you have been talking to Alex about myself,' Jade said to the stunned couple, trying to keep her anger in check. 'Now I'd like to know just exactly what you think of me and what exactly you've been saying about me,' she said, turning up the volume. 'I am not happy.'

'You can say that again,' Jonny muttered. So Jade did. Again and again.

After realising that she wasn't getting anywhere with Kate and Jonny, Jade decided to turn her attention on Alex – and another top 10 entrant in the all-time *Big Brother* hall of fame was born. Jade was incoherent, Alex incandescent. The exact text of the row can't really be described in pleasant company. But suffice it to say that much of what Alex was shouting about involved tongues, kisses and the licking of parts of the housemate's anatomy where the sun doesn't usually shine. It also involved some pretty graphic demonstrations of the body parts in question when Alex rolled over and pulled down his boxer shorts as a visual aid.

'This is about you and me, and about the huge gaping chasm that's in the middle of your face,' he shouted later on, as Jade tried to persuade him to join her in the living room to confront the others. 'Take your crybaby little arse to bed. I really don't have any time for a girl like you. Same as Sandy, if I ever see you again it will be far too soon. You should have been out of here a long, long time ago. I've lost my tolerance of certain things and you're one of them, Jade,' was his final drunken salvo.

While accusations of back-stabbing continued to be made the following morning, the hungover housemates soon managed to create another uneasy truce. Sadly for Jade, however, the other four decided that the best way for them to bond was to play a few tricks on their young housemate. Their favourite was to hide from her.

Tim, Alex, Jonny and Kate disappeared when she was in the bathroom, the Diary Room and the bedroom. 'Why do you always do this to me?' she cried mournfully to the empty rooms as she paced around trying to find them all. 'Hello, *Big Brother*, I don't know where my housemates are,' she said pitifully in the Diary Room at one point when the joke was wearing a little thin. 'Nobody wants to play the game with me. Why wouldn't I be fun to play with?'

Perhaps unaware of the effect this could have on someone as insecure as Jade, the in-crowd had already been ready to rub salt in her wounds by excluding her from other things as well. 'Follow the Van', using a glow-in-the-dark toy van that Alex had found in a Sugar Puffs packet, was a case in point. In what was basically a sex game, Alex and various companions would get under a duvet and drive the little plastic van over their bodies. 'You're not holding my van, you're holding my man,' cried Alex at one point, which gave a bit of a clue about what was really going on.

Kate and Adele had all become pretty good at Alex's little game. But Jade didn't even get to come close to it. 'Am I allowed to play Follow the Van sometime before I go?' she asked finally, putting on a mock baby voice from the bedroom one day. But, while she was trying to joke about it, there were real fears behind the attempts at humour. Once again she knew that she had been excluded and left out of the party. She wasn't really sure why. But it hurt, the way it always did.

'Jade is the most jealous of the housemates. She doesn't like it when she's not in on the game,' said the housemates one night after another Follow the Van game had taken place without her. Without really realising it, they had hit the nail firmly on the head.

Outside the house, viewers had started to notice all these minor cruelties – though as no one could contact the housemates there was nothing anyone could do to try and put them right. 'I felt quite angry at some of the housemates at times because I thought Jade was being given a really hard time and no one would stick up for her,' said Davina McCall when she was asked to look back on the highs and the lows of that year's show. 'Even though they might not have been her best friends, somebody needed to champion her.'

To make matters worse, the games that Jade did get to

play in the house also seemed to be designed at least in part to show her up. Charades isn't something most Bermondsey girls play much at home, as Alex soon realised. 'I've got Jade on my team. I won't get anywhere,' he complained, when he worked out who would be playing with him.

'Half the time I don't really know what you're all talking about and I want the ground to swallow me up so often because of the way people make me feel,' Jade said one day when she had been mocked yet again because of her lack of education.

Her insecurity wasn't exactly helped on Day 63 when the four remaining housemates' daily task was to practise elocution and conversational skills for a series of social etiquette and role-play exercises. Of course, the *Big Brother* producers knew this would make fantastic viewing, as poor Jade was the least polished housemate they had ever had on the show. And right on cue she struggled even to read out the instructions to the group, let alone to thrive in the games themselves.

'An after-dinner speech should always be probably researched and planned,' she began falteringly.

'Properly rehearsed and planned,' corrected Jonny at her side.

'Accordiates are always good, especially if you are the better of the jokes,' she continued.

'Anecdotes are always good, especially if you are the butt of the jokes,' translated Jonny.

'Be ready for herkles and use jesters,' Jade continued.

'Be ready for hecklers and use gestures,' pitched in Jonny, before taking over the rest of the reading.

At first Jade was excited about the big dinner and the games they were going to have to play. 'It will learn me how to speak properly,' she ventured hopefully. But later on her confidence had faded.

'I think I'll be quiet tonight because I find it hard to pronounce all my letters,' Jade said, smiling, just before their final posh meal began. And, while the verbal part of the evening wasn't much fun, Jade, and all the others, certainly looked a million dollars. They had been given evening clothes to wear – Jade's was a fantastically elegant dress held up by tiny shoulder straps, and her long and extravagantly sparkling earrings matched the equally classy necklace *Big Brother* had picked for her.

And so the final morning of the nine-week programme dawned. It was Friday, 26 July and, apart from some light tidying up and half-hearted packing, there was very little to do except wait for the live final that evening. Former housemates say it is hard for viewers to really imagine just how slowly days like these pass when you are trapped in a single compound with no television, telephone, radio, books or newspapers to distract you. 'It's like being in space,' Jade said. 'You can't imagine it till you've experienced it.'

Other former housemates say the silence itself ultimately becomes oppressive. You can walk from one room to another. You can sit down, stand up, lie on your bed. You can go outside and look at the sky. But you are powerless to do anything else. And you certainly can't make the clock tick any faster.

For days the housemates hadn't been able to stop

thinking about what might be going on over the compound's high walls. 'I wonder whether I still have a job?' Jade asked Jonny as they realised that this unique two-month holiday from real life was drawing to a close. 'It's scary, now that it's coming to an end. I don't know what anyone thinks of me. I might have no family and no friends.' More than most, Jade also started to worry about how the newspapers might have portrayed her – though in her worst nightmares she couldn't have guessed the truth.

On the final, nerve-wracking day, however, she managed to put this out of her mind and started to feel a little better. She could focus on getting her striking pale-pink eviction outfit ready. Checking through her silver suitcase on Day 64, she could hardly remember the last time she had packed it – just after the awful arguments with Adele in Week 4, when she had threatened to follow Sunita's lead and walk out of the house of her own accord.

All her official warnings and strikes for gossiping too much about nominations were also pretty much forgotten. The five weird minutes on the first day, when a technical fault had left her locked in the Diary Room, cut off from the rest of the housemates, were just a memory. And she couldn't quite remember what had seemed so important back on Day 6 when she had spent a series record of 31 minutes alone in the Diary Room bending the producers' ears and not letting *Big Brother* get a word in edgeways.

Unknown to Jade, however, the public could remember all of her emotional highs and lows. And everyone was increasingly starting to remember them fondly. 'Jade has single-handedly supplied the nation with more entertainment, shocks and irritations than the rest of the inmates put together,' said television presenter Vanessa Feltz, trying to drum up support for the girl. 'We have watched her waistline and her temper grow. She's a one-off, the grit in the oyster without which there will be no pearl.'

Putting the huge rows and the infamous strip aside, Vanessa said Jade's biggest contribution to the year's entertainment industry were what would be called her 'Jade-isms'. Many of these have since turned into urban legend, exaggerated or slightly modified to fit a new series of stories or jokes. But the best of them are as funny today as they were back in 2002.

Early on Alex called Jade 'a sandwich short of a picnic', and food and drink did appear to be one area where Jade's education was a little rough around the edges. 'What's a sparagus?' she asked when the conversation got round to recipes one day. Asked in the Diary Room to name two vegetables that begin with the letter 'S', she came up with the inspired answer 'Strawberries and spinach'. When told this was wrong, she came up with 'Spinach and spuds', as a hopeful alternative.

Then there were her thoughts on food hygiene: 'If you don't cook the yellow bits of eggs you get semolina.' And her taste for the good life: 'I like that pink champagne, Don Perrier,' she said, convinced she could fit in among the super-rich and the jet set.

Surprisingly enough, even popular culture was a struggle for her. 'I look like God's gorilla,' she told Alex one morning after looking at her hair in the mirror and thinking she looked like Godzilla. 'Are they filming us out there? I look like a state.'

After falling about laughing following a disastrous attempt to get fit on the running machine, Jade proved that, while she might enjoy other physical activities, she wasn't that good at describing them. 'I love optical courses,' she declared, before moving on to the animal kingdom. 'I don't want to be your escape goat,' she shouted during one argument, effectively inventing a whole new animal. She also thought chickens ate cheese and asked if the circles on male peacock's feathers really were their eyes. And outside the house, before going on Graham Norton's chat show, she famously asked if a ferret was a bird.

Meanwhile, she said she thought the fictional Inspector Morse was related to the very real Mother Teresa and that Sherlock Holmes was a true-life policeman. Next up was her theory that whodunnit author Agatha Christie was in fact the figure from Greek legend who flew too close to the sun and had his wings burned. Add 'Heinzstein' to the mix and it's clear that history had never been Jade's best subject in school. 'In the olden days they had wirelephones and they got music off that,' she hazarded one day when the group were being driven mad by the silence in the house.

Jade's geographical gaffes would become equally famous. 'Rio de Janeiro, ain't that a person?' was one of the best. 'Was Lynne Scottish?' she also asked, amazed, after the Aberdeen girl with the strong Scottish accent had left the house. Jade also wanted to check that people spoke English in America before considering going there, and then queried, 'Do they speak Portuganese in Portugal?' before following up with 'I thought Portugal was in Spain.'

National and city boundaries weren't her strong point either. 'The Union Jack is for all of us. But the St George is just for London, isn't it?' she hazarded. And then there was her famous, tortuous conversation with Spencer about his famous and historic hometown – about which Jade knew very little.

'I'm confused, I thought Cambridge was in London. I knew Birmingham weren't in London,' she began when he was talking about his job on the River Cam. 'I thought it was just a bit out. In London, but a bit out. You know, you've got Bermondsey, Lewisham and all them sort of places. I thought that Cambridge was in London but in a different place.'

'Cambridge is a city,' explained Spencer, hoping that this might ring some bells.

'But we've got the city in London,' Jade replied, with impeccable logic.

'Yes, the city is called London and there're different parts of it. Cambridge is a city,' Spencer followed up.

'Of where? Kent?' questioned Jade, her mind racing. 'Well, England's a country, London's a city, Bermondsey's just a throw-off. Now where are you? What's your country and what's your things? I'm confused.'

You could say that again, Jade. Spencer tried to make things clear. 'What country am I from? England,' he said finally and with emphasis. 'The city is called Cambridge. The county is called Cambridgeshire.'

'So it's not Kent then?' Jade checked.

'No, the region is called East Anglia.'

'East Angular? That's abroad. Is there not a place called East Angular abroad?'

'Jade, have you been taking the stupid pills again?' Spencer famously asked, amazed.

But Jade was determined to prove that she might still be right about this whole geography-nationality thing. 'Every time people tell me they work in East Angular, I actually think they are talking about near Tunisia and places like that. Am I thick?'

Spencer kindly didn't comment. And Jade wasn't finished. Her thought processes were getting ever further off the wall. 'Because Scottish and Irish and all that comes under England, doesn't it?' she questioned, apropos nothing in particular.

'No. They come under Great Britain,' said the long-suffering Spencer. 'Scotland and Wales have their own flags. Northern Ireland and Ireland are different.'

'So they're not together? Where's Berlin?' And so it went on.

In retrospect, it is little wonder that several papers only half-jokingly demanded the resignation of the Government's Education Minister as each new Jade-ism hit the headlines. Or that someone else thought she should try and get elected as Prime Minister when the show was over. 'She doesn't listen to a word anyone says, has no idea what is going on in the country, and just generally lives on a planet of her own. Politics has to be the answer for her,' was the pretty sound conclusion on the official online *Big Brother* fan site.

But in the final analysis it was clear that the butt of most of Jade's jokes and mistakes was usually herself. Constantly referring to herself as a 'chipstick', she single-handedly added that word to the nation's vocabulary in 2002. And she was always happy to own up to her limitations. 'I've been wracking my brains out and I ain't got much to wrack,' she admitted to Spencer during a conversation about politics. For all that, there were also times when Jade proved to be as quick-witted as anyone else in the house. For example, one night Alex had been trying to tell her she didn't have the intelligence to see how the others were manipulating her to avoid eviction nominations. 'Jade, you're just a dental nurse,' he told her dismissively.

'Oh, sorry, Mr Model,' she fired back without missing a beat.

And for all the laughter that her various gaffes and Jade-isms caused – and all the mileage that the papers and comedians would get out of them – some would turn out to be sadly prophetic. One question in particular still stands out: 'What does hostile mean?' Jade asked in the early days of the programme when everyone was still having fun.

Little did she know that, when she walked back into the real world to read the newspaper headlines nine weeks later, she was going to find out. With a vengeance.

chapter 6

So Thanks,
Graham Norton

Singing a few lines from a song, cooking meals, gossiping, taking part in the challenges, laughing, drinking and joking. Locked away inside the Big Brother house, Jade had absolutely no idea about what was going on in the outside world. She didn't know if she was popular or unpopular; if she was being loved, hated or ignored; if her fellow housemates were getting all the attention and she was being forgotten. She didn't know if anyone was really watching the show or if anyone was talking about it.

She certainly didn't know that she had become the most infamous new face in Britain.

Before going into the house, *Big Brother* producers warned Jade that she might get some 'negative attention' for being 'ditzy and blonde' on the show. If only the world had been that kind.

The insults thrown at Jade were far more personal and

hurtful. The sheer scale of the coverage was staggering. And the ferocity of the attacks on Jade – just 20 when she entered the house – was extraordinary. Not since Fergie was derided as the 'Duchess of Pork' has a woman been so ridiculed for her figure and her appearance.

Looking back, the brutal descriptions almost take your breath away. 'Pig Brother' and 'Big Blubber' were two of the softest headlines above Jade's photos in the tabloids. She was described as 'a slug-like beast' and 'a vile fishwife with the hideous head of a pig' in the *Mirror*. The *Sun* branded her 'the oinker' and 'the most hated woman in Britain', while columnist Garry Bushell declared, 'She's horrible – foul of mouth and flabby of belly.'

The *Daily Mail* called her 'foul-mouthed' and 'the living embodiment of the phrase dumbing down', before asking, 'How can a person so thick get through life?' What the papers seemed to forget was that Jade was nothing more than an insecure 20-year-old when she applied to go on the show. And once inside the *Big Brother* house she was unable to fight back because she had no idea what was going on.

Beyond the aggressive headlines the more detailed descriptions of Jade were just as bad. 'If you took Sharon Mitchell, the former landlady of the Queen Vic in *EastEnders*, and blew her up with a bicycle pump until you couldn't pump any more, then you'd have Jade,' said far-from-skinny columnist Allison Pearson in the London *Evening Standard* – in an article written to support her.

And was Jade's heart-rending drunken strip really bad enough to justify this, from the *Daily Mirror*? 'We saw fat-rolled, Michelin girl Jade in all her preposterous lack of glory. Naked as the day Dr Frankenstein made her. Mothers should cover their children's eyes – and their own. A pig lookalike unveiling cascading mountains of blubber while downing industrial quantities of wine.' To this day it is hard to imagine how you would feel reading this about yourself – in an age when the body beautiful is admired above almost everything else.

To make matters worse, the media's attacks were being lapped up by the general public. Outside the Elstree studio, crowds turned up every night bringing placards and banners saying, 'Kill the Pig', 'Slaughter the Pig' – a disturbing echo of the climactic scenes in the William Golding novel *Lord of the Flies*, where the boys use the same rallying calls as they round on the hated fat boy in their midst, smash his glasses and signal the breakdown of decent, human behaviour.

Nothing so dramatic happened outside the *Big Brother* house in 2002. But with the crowd unfurling new banners saying, 'Jade – Go to Hell' and 'This Little Piggy Should Go Home', there were real worries that it might, especially considering the crowd's long-standing hostility. When the show's host Davina McCall interviewed the housemates evicted in the first few weeks of the series, the crowd erupted in boos and jeers every time anyone mentioned Jade's name, or whenever her face appeared on the giant video screens. It made gripping, must-see television, which was just what the show's producers were banking on. But the cruelty of mob rule was undeniable.

Ironically enough, all this was happening in Elstree TV

and Film Studios in Hertfordshire, where what feels like a million years ago they had filmed that most gentle of British dramas *The Railway Children*. In 2002 Jade Goody was to find out just how much Britain had changed since then.

She was also going to discover that the attacks on her respected no social, educational or gender lines. Germaine Greer – supposedly a feminist – appeared to have no solidarity with poor Jade, for example. 'That fat slag deserves all she gets,' the writer and academic was reported to have declared just before the filming of her *Newsnight Review* show began one night. Words that might come back to haunt her nearly three years later when Germaine shocked her fans by entering the 2005 *Celebrity Big Brother* contest alongside other luminaries such as Caprice, Brigitte Nielsen, John McCririck and Jeremy Edwards.

Interestingly enough, Germaine unwittingly showed that the girl she had allegedly attacked was a stronger character than she herself would prove to be. Jade, of course, stayed in the house to the final day of the nine-week competition. Germaine couldn't cope with the pressure or with what she perceived to be the rudeness of some of her fellow housemates, so she walked out after just five days.

Other people who should have known better were equally cruel. Brian Sewell, the urbane and well-educated art critic of the London *Evening Standard*, wrote, 'Jade is the most raucous, obtrusive, inconsiderate, graceless and immature, not only of the women, but of the whole group, and with the looks of something pupped by a Japanese fighting dog from the Dong with the luminous nose.'

Things actually got worse as the weeks went by. 'Vote out the pig!' demanded the *Sun* in headlines over full-page articles, giving the 09011 number to encourage readers to call to evict Jade from the show. 'Ditch the witch!' screamed the *People*, laying into 'the dental nurse who can't keep her own gob shut'. And, of course, all the papers illustrated the articles with some of the least flattering pictures of Jade – shots of her yawning openly, putting her fist in her mouth as a joke, squeezing spots or making faces in the mirrors. And the reporters didn't even try to excuse their actions or apologise for what they were doing. 'Life will be hard for Jade when she leaves the house,' said the *Sun*'s show-business columnist Dominic Mohan. 'But don't feel sorry for her. Exercise your democratic right and vote the pig out.'

Other senior journalists were equally candid about why they saw Jade as fair game – and why they thought that readers wanted her in the papers. 'She was blonde, she was large and had big boobs,' offered *Daily Sport* editor Tony Livesey with refreshing honesty. 'She was the most stupid person you could ever meet,' thought the *Daily Mirror*'s Kevin O'Sullivan, while former *People*, Neil Wallis admitted that Jade was a character made in tabloid heaven. 'If all that wasn't enough, she had a one-armed lesbian mother. You could not have invented that,' he said.

With hindsight, it is obvious that simple sexism and snobbery played at least some part in the attacks. It was Jade, for example, rather than PJ, who took the flak for what might or might not have happened under the trainee solicitor's sheets on Day 20. The male-dominated media's view seemed to be that PJ's crime had simply been an understandable lapse from a man who would normally have known better. Jade, however, was roundly condemned as a slapper.

It didn't even seem to bother the papers that the well-educated lawyer proved himself to be no gentleman. Even before he famously cold-shouldered her in the summer's most excruciating attempted hug, PJ had told the other housemates, 'I was just pissed out of my face, I don't even fancy her. People probably hate me now because I pulled Jade.'

The papers took PJ's excuse about being drunk seriously. Two of them commissioned national opinion polls to find out, 'How drunk would you have to be to have sex with Jade?' Sadly for her, the overwhelming answer was 'very'. And PJ himself called her a '10-pinter' in later interviews.

Jade's soon-to-be ex-boyfriend Danny also heaped on the pressure. 'She's a sex-crazed, lying, two-timing, drunken tart, and I hope I never see her again,' he told the papers, full of righteous indignation. 'I was totally in love with Jade and adored her but she has hurt me in the worst way possible.' But he did have a final dig, just to keep his paymasters on the papers happy, by saying she was an 'insatiable' lover who enjoyed outdoor sex.

Amazingly enough, Jade, who was to have to forgive an awful lot of people for an awful lot of things when she got back in the real world, was also able to see Danny's point of view. 'I don't blame him,' she said magnanimously. 'He must have felt totally humiliated and I am sorry for that.'

Nevertheless, while she was still in the *Big Brother* house her family were increasingly worried about her welfare.

'The producers were told that they had to tread carefully with this girl,' said her aunt, Michelle Craddock. 'She survived a childhood which could easily have left her damaged and she should be pulled out because the world is being really nasty to her. She could hang herself because of what people are saying.'

'I can't stand seeing my daughter treated this way,' said mum Jackiey. 'I just want to jump into the telly and bring her home. It's torture every time I switch on the TV or hear someone talking about her and I'm terrified she will get lynched when she gets out.'

And at one point this did look very likely. During the course of the show a 15-year-old schoolgirl was beaten up by her classmates – her crime being to look just a little bit like poor Jade. 'Mothers across the country can point to Jade and say to their daughters, "If you don't watch out, you might grow up to be like her,"' was the view of the *Daily Mail*, which said Jade's name was 'a byword for stupidity and ugliness'.

But, as the attacks intensified, questions were finally being asked about whether we were seeing and judging the real Jade – or whether she was being manipulated and demonised by the show's production team in search of ratings and publicity. Critics said the *Big Brother* producers were clearly guilty of encouraging Jade to do things she would almost certainly regret when the series was over.

'I don't think Jade should have been fuelled with alcohol and allowed to strip naked,' says Melanie Hill, who was booed by the crowds when she had left the first ever *Big Brother* house in 2000, and has been a respected commentator on the reality-TV phenomenon ever since. 'Jade needed protection but, in the battle for ratings, perhaps the vulnerability of some contestants doesn't matter. People in the series need to know that their 15 minutes of fame will come at a very high price.'

Other broadcasters agreed. Wayne Garvie, head of BBC Entertainment Production, asked whether the *Big Brother* producers had been deliberately exploiting Jade and said her drunken strip was 'nothing less than the gross exploitation of a vulnerable woman by a group of drunken men'.

By coincidence, Jade's ratings-topping strip (stills of which were among the most widely sought images on the Internet that summer) had been seen just after an equally worrying public display from football's former golden boy Paul Gascoigne. Gazza was trying his hand as a pundit for the summer's World Cup coverage and it wasn't going well. He looked hungover and was clearly nervous on his first appearance under the studio lights.

'The car crash that was Gazza's World Cup punditry saw an equally troubled man hung out to dry in the studio, his disarray compounded when the tabloids reported the excesses of his minibar,' Garvie said. 'Are Jade and Gazza willing participants in their own theatre of cruelty, or is it a dereliction of duty by producers on behalf of unstable people?'

Jade, interestingly enough, was determined not to push any blame for her behaviour on to others when she looked back on her nine alcohol-fuelled weeks in the house. 'There would have been just as much fun without the alcohol and *Big Brother* didn't exactly force-feed us the booze. We were put in there for the individuals that we were and we knew what was going on,' she said.

But on a different level questions were also being asked about the way *Big Brother* producers had manipulated the vast amount of footage they recorded in the show's first few weeks to build Jade up as such a huge hate figure – then to move the focus elsewhere to ensure she wasn't in fact evicted.

'The producers realised Jade was good box office and are desperately manipulating the format of the show to keep her from being voted off,' said one television reviewer as the first few gripping weeks of the show unfolded.

Former *Big Brother* contestants suggested that telly bosses were trying to take the heat off Jade in case she had a mental breakdown or was beaten up after leaving the house. 'It was obvious Jade would be in for a bad time if she came out that week,' said *Big Brother* anti-hero Nick Bateman, who had famously been thrown out of the first series of the show for alleged cheating. 'So suddenly they started editing it so Adele looked much worse than her. That is the only reason I can think of why Adele would be evicted – the public has always hated Jade the most out of everyone in the house. The producers had fun turning Jade into the bitch of the show, but then I think they realised they had gone too far – and that people hated her so much she could be attacked. They started back-pedalling furiously and made Adele out to be the real two-faced one through clever editing.'

Bateman's theories were soon backed up by the programme's production team. 'All last week's shows were edited to show Adele at her worst and Jade acting a lot quieter,' a *Big Brother* insider told the *Sun*. 'This was a deliberate move to keep Jade in the house because she stirs things up, and to avoid criticism that they have turned her into a monster. Their biggest fear is that a housemate suffers a high-profile breakdown after appearing on the show and then tries to sue.'

Jade, Adele, Jonny and Kate were all up for eviction in the vital sixth week when critics said the clever editing had begun. But as all the polls suggested Jonny and Kate were only getting a tiny number of eviction votes, the real battle was between Jade and Adele – and in the end Jade came out on top. More than 3.4 million eviction votes were cast, another new record for this stage of the show. And against all the odds and all expectations Adele got 2.1 million, or more than 60 per cent of them, and left the house that night.

Jade had survived to live another day in the *Big Brother* house – and to attract ever-more ugly and irresponsible coverage in the media. In the worst days even those who tried to defend Jade were unable to do so wholeheartedly. At one point the *Daily Star* ran a campaign to stop the attacks, but the paper called it, 'Save Miss Piggy's bacon'. The *Sunday Mirror* had a similarly mixed message. 'All the pig references are just plain insulting – to pigs,' it declared.

Former contestants said that Jade should have expected her bad press, and wouldn't have a leg to stand on if she complained about it. 'Once you go into that show, you sign your life away,' said Nick Bateman. 'Jade and all the other contestants have seen two series of what it is like in *Big Brother* and should not have been naïve enough to think they would come out smelling of roses. So I can't have that much sympathy for Jade now.'

However, Paul Ferguson (who had been in Series 2 under the name Bubble) offered a little more perspective. 'I equate going on the show with putting your hand on a table and saying, "Hit it with a hammer." You know it is going to hurt but you don't know how much until they hit you. Whatever you imagine it to be, multiply it by 10 and it's worse.'

Other commentators were also starting to agree that the ferocity and quantity of the attacks on Jade couldn't in fact have been anticipated. And after a while some more genuine support appeared to be building up for the *Big Brother* baby – the show's youngest ever competitor.

Vanessa Feltz, no stranger to attacks about her own figure, offered some support by trying to retain a sense of perspective about the situation. 'Jade's ignorance is breathtaking,' she began her commentary. 'Her self-obsession, repetition, flair for inanities and tendency to sing loudly to fill any vacuum of silence have stunned the nation. She's silly, annoying and stultifying company, but let's not go overboard here. Jade is basically a good-natured girl in an unnatural and hugely demanding environment. She hasn't committed any crimes or hanging offences. Mercy for Jade.'

Sarah Dempster, television editor of the *Scotsman*, was even more supportive. 'If anyone else had suffered the levels of abuse hurled at Jade, they would be cowering under a snooker table in a psychiatric hospital with a man claiming to be Henry VIII. Jade is a woman so impervious to the slights and slurs of misogynistic journalists that she deserves a medal.' Amazingly, campaigns to reduce the attacks on Jade even took off on the other side of the world. The respected *Melbourne Age* newspaper in Australia criticised 'the barrage of abuse directed against her which generated a level of hostility usually reserved for child murderers'.

Back in Bermondsey itself, there was also a sense that the whole community was under attack – and that Jade deserved a break. Local band The Reason had an end-of-show gig including their specially written track 'Big Brother (A Song for Jade)' and the *South London Press* launched a Savejade.com website for supporters. Meanwhile, local MP Simon Hughes said public opinion in his constituency was fully supportive. 'I have not met anyone in Bermondsey who isn't backing Jade to stay in the house and win. Jade has made a big impact on the show in every way and people in Bermondsey will stand by her, whatever happens,' he said.

Other commentators spotted occasional acts of selfless kindness on Jade's part, which were being ignored as the rush to attack her got ever stronger. On Day 61, for example, Jade was the only housemate who stayed sober in the latest of the show's marathon drinking sessions. She then cleaned up the house, comforted the drunken Kate and helped Jonny to bed.

'She was also the only one of the housemates who ventured out in the pouring rain to clean out the chickens,' noted deputy editor of the *TV Times* Roger Felton. 'That too proved she's got a heart and is not just in it for herself.' Felton also correctly predicted that the unprecedented abuse heaped upon Jade and the shabby treatment she was getting inside the house would trigger a belated backlash. 'When she lost the stripping game, it was as if she had been set up by the boys and that didn't make comfortable viewing. Women will also feel sympathetic to her over the way PJ treated her. Jade is the underdog who claws her way back into contention.'

Seeing the other housemates play tricks on the 21-year-old and exclude her from their games also had an effect on viewers, according to *Big Brother* psychiatrist Dr Sandra Scott. 'When the media turned on Jade and she was vilified in much of the press this introduced another factor – the audience's sense of fair play. Right or wrong, it was not fair for Jade to be punished inside and outside the house. Whatever her crimes, the fact that everyone ganged up on Jade looked like bullying,' she said.

Other media commentators said Jade was in effect being attacked for being herself – in a room full of fakes. 'Jade has been loud, drunk, coarse and ignorant, but none of these things would raise many eyebrows on her native Old Kent Road on a Saturday night,' said television writer John Morrish of the *Independent on Sunday*. 'Jade's crime, or her misfortune, has been to behave like that while other contestants were prettier and better groomed: and that was just the men.'

Veteran anthropologist Desmond Morris, author of books such as *The Human Zoo*, was also ready to give Jade some light-hearted comfort. First of all, he said neither she nor her other housemates were as stupid as they looked. 'The truth is that the *Big Brother* inmates are not imbeciles but simply ordinary people placed in an imbecilic situation,' he said fairly. Then, for reasons that seem to have since been forgotten, Morris decided to compare each of the main housemates to dogs.

Kate, typically, got the softest ride. 'She is the delightful golden retriever, so attractive that it is hard to understand why she is moping in the corner of the stress-laden enclosure instead of prancing down a sun-kissed beach chasing sticks thrown by her besotted owners,' Morris decided. PJ was faintly damned as 'a cheerfully scruffy, randy bull terrier', while Jonny was 'a retired rescue dog, so highly trained to be helpful that he is now constantly worried about his inability to perform inside the dog house.'

And good old Jade? According to Morris, she was 'the galumphing, big-mouthed Rottweiler who was such a pampered puppy that she grew up thinking she was a little lapdog and can't help causing havoc by repeatedly reverting to type'.

Very slowly others were taking a similarly sympathetic view of Jade and many of those who had been tormenting her the most throughout the first few weeks of the show had changed their opinions as it drew to a close. In Week 8 Graham Norton, for example, was asked whom of the final four contestants he was rooting for.

'I'd love it if Jade won,' he said, having derided her mercilessly for the past two months. 'She's really put the work in, while the other three have played the game to a certain extent. She has cried and screamed her way through, and she's been by far the most entertaining person in there. I'm just really fond of her. She's the poor cow that everyone picks on. You feel very protective of her.' Graham, to his credit, was happy to admit that his current opinions would surprise anyone who heard his earlier rants about how awful Jade was. 'A lot of people have changed their opinion on Jade,' he said. 'It's like living next to the railway – annoying at first but you'd miss it once it's gone.'

And the star had one more thing to say – the most important thing of all. 'I'd love to get Jade on my show,' he proclaimed. 'She's the only one of the four I will ask.' Fortunately for her, Graham would prove to be true to his word. Jade wouldn't just go on his show once, she would appear every day in the first week after her eviction – unprecedented for any of his celebrity guests before or since. And this would boot her firmly towards the celebrity stratosphere she had always been dreaming about.

But before this, there were more indignities and cruelties to suffer, more insults to face. Take the *Mail on Sunday*'s description of Jade being asked questions at her first post-eviction press conference – when the 21-year-old was tired and terrified in equal measure. 'Jade, her ample figure crammed into a pink satin dress that resembled a giant sausage skin, looked panic-stricken,' wrote journalists Louisa Pritchard and Nick Pryer. 'Her chubby arms began flapping wildly, her eyes rolled and she started squawking, "arrgh, arrgh, dunno, dunno," in her South London foghorn of a voice that one commentator likened to a never-ending migraine.'

The *Mirror*, meanwhile, didn't think that her dress looked like a giant sausage skin at all. 'A kind of pink satin marquee' was its sensitive, fashion-conscious verdict. And it wasn't just Jade's dress sense that was under attack as the show drew to a close. Brian Sewell, in the *Evening Standard*, even took a potshot at her name. He wrote that she had been 'fortuitously christened' as the word jade had been 'slang for a hussy since the days of Chaucer'.

Jade's prospects back in the real world were also bleak – according to the media. London's *Evening Standard* newspaper said her employment options were 'probably limited to appearances on *Teletubbies*, on Harry Enfield's show as Tim Nice-But-Dim's common girlfriend or as a bouncy castle at Thorpe Park'. Meanwhile, bookies took bets that her first job after *Big Brother* would be a guest slot on *The Muppet Show* but not as herself – as a Muppet.

Even so, Jade at least pretended to take all the criticism and the insults in her stride. 'I never knew about it all till I came out of the house,' she said afterwards. 'I didn't even read the coverage. The first thing I saw was a thing with my picture next to Bin Laden – we were the two most hated people in the world, they said.'

Previous *Big Brother* hate figures say that the show's producers deliberately keep the bad press from contestants for at least a day so they can get through the essential post-show press conferences without breaking down. Melanie Hill, who made it to the final four in the first series of *Big Brother*, explains how it works. 'On the night of my eviction I wasn't remotely worried,' she says. 'I was so looking forward to seeing my mum and my friends that I couldn't wait to pack. When I walked out into the bright lights I was excited and a bit nervous. And then I heard people booing me. I couldn't believe it – what had I done?'

The *Big Brother* production team weren't to tell her for quite some time. Mel says the live post-eviction interview with Davina went by 'in an adrenaline-fuelled flash' and that she was then 'whisked away to a grotty Portakabin to face endless discussions with various producers about what would happen to me over the next couple of days.

'It wasn't until two hours after the show had finished that I was allowed to see my ex-boyfriend, who was going to stay the night with me in a secret hotel in London. By this time all my friends and family had gone home and I hadn't even seen my mum.'

The next morning Mel got an inkling of what was going on. She decided to go and buy some hair conditioner – and found that two bodyguards were on hand to accompany her out of the hotel and across the street to Superdrug. 'I couldn't understand why I needed protection, and I began to feel as claustrophobic as I had in the house,' she says. 'Later that day I was seen by the show's psychiatrist. He warned me that the press would ask about how much I had flirted inside the house, but didn't give me any advice on how to cope. I was sat down with a press officer, who coached me in the art of avoiding awkward questions. He said, "You came across as a bit of a maneater, Mel."'

Mel, then 26, who had only ever had five relationships in her life and had always been faithful, was starting to panic. And still no one seemed ready to help her or explain why this was all happening. 'During that first weekend out of the house I was shunted from one stranger to another, I wasn't allowed to go home, and I was starting to feel anxious and lonely.

'At the press conference the next day I was asked, "How does it feel being labelled the black widow and the praying mantis?" I thought, what the hell are they talking about? It started to dawn on me that something sinister was going on. I began to panic and wanted more than anything to go home. What had my mum gone through and what was she thinking? I still hadn't been allowed to see what had been written in the papers about me.'

Of course, the column inches and the criticism aimed at former Information Technology worker Mel in 2000 were nothing compared with those aimed at Jade two years later. Interestingly enough, 26 July 2002, the final day of *Big Brother 3*, turned out to be a particularly poignant anniversary as well.

A look through the history books shows this was the 140th anniversary of the birth of John Merrick. In his adult life Merrick was to be known as the Elephant Man – and his story, though not his looks, bears uncanny similarities with that of Jade Goody more than a hundred years later.

Merrick was raised in poverty by a single parent. He was the victim of what is now known as neurofibromatosis – an awful, painful and disfiguring illness that contorted his features and made his face and head look particularly grotesque. At a young age he was desperate to escape his life of poverty and achieve something. So Merrick volunteered to join the *Big Brother* of his day – the fairground freak show run by infamously cruel circus manager Sam Torr.

Merrick celebrated – if that is the right word – his 21st birthday on public display in one of Torr's show tents. He came of age as a money-making exhibit, mocked, tormented, laughed at and loathed by the paying public. Anyone who doesn't think this sounds familiar should watch the 1980 film *The Elephant Man*, directed by *Twin Peaks* creator David Lynch and starring the Oscar-nominated John Hurt as Merrick.

In the film Merrick enjoyed a happy ending, of sorts. A doctor intervened one day when a mob had gathered to stone Merrick near London's Liverpool Street Station. Dr Frederick Treves, played by Anthony Hopkins, rescued the bleeding young man and gave him refuge in the London Hospital in nearby Whitechapel. There, Merrick was treated with kindness and love for the first time in his short life. He became a favourite of the nursing staff and was visited by royalty. Would Jade Goody, who had suffered such public derision at the same age as Merrick, ever find her own Dr Treves?

At first it looked unlikely, because the personal assaults on her continued long after she left the *Big Brother* house. And even the playful attacks must have hurt someone as sensitive about her appearance as Jade. At one point a *Sun* reporter, for example, decided to ring up a series of top dress designers pretending to be Jade's personal assistant. He asked if she could borrow one of their gowns for the upcoming MTV Music Awards. Designers normally fall over themselves to offer free dresses to the stars so they can get some valuable publicity and be forever linked in the public's mind with the rich, famous and glamorous. But the

Sun gleefully reported that the staff at Gucci, Chanel, John Paul Gaultier, Chloe and every other designer it approached had all said that, if Jade wanted to wear their clothes, she would have to pay full price for the privilege.

As for the future, the experts were starting to worry about the long-term effects of Jade's unprecedented journey through the highs and lows of the modern media. Cynthia McVey is a psychologist at Glasgow Caledonian University who has carried out several studies of reality TV and worked on *Castaway 2000* for the BBC. She said, 'It will be difficult for Jade in the outside world because the campaign against her has gone across all the key elements: her looks, her brains and her personality. If people only criticise one of these, then you can say, "Well, at least I'm good-looking" or "At least I'm brainy." But she's been under attack on all three. It will be a baptism of fire and a horrible experience for her. She will need the support of her family and friends, and all the psychological support that Channel 4 will give her.'

So should the whole *Big Brother* experiment have taken place at all? David Wilson, professor of criminology at the University of Central England in Birmingham, was wary, saying the whole concept deliberately encourages unnecessary and dangerous conflict. 'I would never be able to do this as an academic piece of research. An ethics committee would say it was putting people at risk,' he said.

High-profile media psychologist Oliver James was equally concerned about Jade – and everyone else taking part in reality-TV shows. 'People appearing in factual television shows are far more vulnerable than anyone in the television world will ever admit,' he said. 'A significant proportion of contestants are people who are dissatisfied with their lives, who are unhappy, and who hope that by participating in the show their lives will be changed to some extent.' And James said his research suggested that very few achieved the changes they had hoped for, with most suffering depression as a result. James has campaigned to persuade the television companies that profit so much from reality shows to put more money into support systems for their participants.

In 2002 *Big Brother*'s producers did claim to be ready to help – hopefully having learned from the failings in the system identified by Melanie Hill from Series 1. They said the support was first available long before the filming began and could continue for many months afterwards.

'We try to prepare the contestants as fully as possible for the intense experience of life in the *Big Brother* house and the impact it may have on their lives,' said a Channel 4 spokesperson. 'Contestants have an in-depth psychological screening at least twice before they are finally chosen to enter the house. They are also subjected to a "talk of doom" on several occasions, where producers fully outline all the possible negative aspects of taking part. We actually warn contestants that this could be the worst experience of their lives. And once contestants leave the house we have an aftercare support system in place so that every aspect of their welfare is looked after by professionals. This includes being able to talk to a psychologist, as well as to the production team, about their experience. In light of all this we are fully confident that Jade is up to the challenge of *Big Brother*.'

Big Brother series editor Gigi Eligoloff admitted she was concerned about the way the media was picking on Jade. 'I think it is a shame that there is so much personal criticism of Jade,' she said. 'I also think that Jade has been on a very interesting journey and has learned a lot about herself and perhaps her bad points.' Gigi also denied that the selection of housemates had been made specifically to create tensions. 'It's a complete misconception to suggest that we want people to hate each other and be rowing constantly. Ideally we want people to get on well, to really bond.'

Peter Bazalgette, the millionaire creative director of *Big Brother* production company Endemol, said he completely refuted suggestions that they had only selected Jade out of the 150,000 other *Big Brother* applicants because she was a vulnerable target and would make good television if she cracked up under the pressure. 'That is completely untrue. We wanted a cockney girl, and that's all,' he said.

Big Brother executive producer Phil Edgar-Jones was also keen to say that the anti-Jade campaigns had taken the whole crew by surprise. 'We don't want Jade to become the most hated person in Britain and we think things have gone too far in some cases – for example, her being compared to a pig. Of course, a programme like *Big Brother*, which is in effect an unpopularity contest, causes feelings to run high but we do look after people when they come out of the house. Jade will get to talk to people who can help her.'

Edgar-Jones was also keen to point out that the producers had not put Jade under any pressure they didn't think she was capable of withstanding. 'Like every housemate, she has been through a series of psychological evaluations and we believe she is one of the most robust people – mentally – that we have met.'

Thankfully for Jade, he was right. She had experienced enough knocks in her short life to be ready for those the media had thrown at her. 'Because the life I have had has been quite tough, I took everything with a pinch of salt. I'd been through such a difficult time as a child that anything written about me wasn't going to make me kill myself. I laughed at it all. I'd been through a harder time in real life.'

This was the common-sense attitude that would get Jade through the horror of seeing how she had been portrayed to the world. It was the same common sense that would soon turn her from one of the most hated women in Britain to one of our favourites.

'The first moment I saw Jade I thought she was possibly the most dreadful person I had ever seen,' said *Big Brother's Little Brother* social commentator Jenni Trent-Hughes, who is also a relationship expert on Channel 4's *Perfect Match*. 'But by the end of the series I was trying to get her number to have her round for dinner.'

Jenni wasn't the only one to have undergone such a transformation. Jade Goody, against all the odds, was suddenly in demand.

chapter 7

Kiss and Tell

They all came creeping out of the woodwork long before Jade came out of the Big Brother house. Family, friends, neighbours, past and present boyfriends – everyone lined up to take some cash from the papers in return for some unflattering and often unbelievable kiss-and-tell stories about Jade.

Some days it didn't even seem to matter how ludicrous the allegation was, or how distant the teller's link was to Jade. Journalists were still willing to open their chequebooks and pay for some dirt they could splash all over the front pages.

And, unluckily, Jade's colourful past and extraordinary family meant reporters didn't have to look far to find controversy. So, as the weeks went on, there were ever more stories about the Goodys' financial and legal problems. Stories about all their tortured relationships. And, predictably, stories upon stories about sex. 'Jade is a sex addict!' screamed the *People* in its first weekend of saturation coverage of all things Goody when *Big Brother* had just ended. 'Red-hot Jade revelations,' followed up the next day's *Sun*. 'Saucy secrets about our Jade,' countered the *Star*.

One week on and things hadn't got any quieter in the kiss-and-tell stakes. 'Girl-hungry Jade Goody moaned with ecstasy as she seduced a teenage pal for lesbian sex,' began the *People* in another salacious story in its 'X-rated *Big Brother* special'. And it was always hoping for more. 'Did Jade ever jump you? Tell us your tale of *Big Brother* lust today,' wrote the *People* at the end of the story, before giving the direct line to the paper's ever-ready news desk.

And if former friends couldn't find a sexual story to tell about Jade then almost anything else would do instead. 'Jade bit girl's ear off … and ate it!' proclaimed one of the tabloids the following weekend. There was news about Jade's and her outstanding council tax bills. Then came entirely false stories about the Goody family being thrown out of their homes for bad behaviour towards their neighbours, and bizarre bullying allegations from Jade's schooldays.

The sheer volume of negative publicity meant that Jade could treat the most outlandish stories with the contempt they deserved. She and mum Jackiey were even able to laugh at some of the more ridiculous concoctions, and were advised by the *Big Brother* producers to just sit back, ignore everything and wait for life to get back to normal. At least I am finally being attacked for my actual life and for the things they think I have done, she thought. That's at least a little bit easier to bear than being attacked for what I look like and how much I weigh.

For all that, some reports did genuinely hurt the 21-year-old. And they forced Jade to issue some fierce denials. The first concerned some of her wildest moments in the *Big Brother* house and the inferences people were making from them. 'I might have come across on telly as a bit of a tramp who gets her clothes off when she's drunk. But I'm not a slag at all. I can count the number of men I have slept with on one hand and I have never, ever, had a one-night stand. I know some things I did in the house made me look like a right slapper, but I am not,' she told reporters firmly when she finally had her chance to give her side of the Jade Goody story.

And while it might not seem to matter too much in the overall scheme of things, Jade was also upset by some tabloid stories saying she had snubbed her family and friends since leaving the *Big Brother* house. One paper said she hadn't gone back to her old home once since finding fame, that she had only briefly spoken to mum Jackiey on the phone rather than in person, and that she was spending too much time and money in posh West End shops and nightclubs. They said she was getting too big-headed and was obsessed with money and new celebrity friends.

In reality, these rumours were completely false. In public, as well as in private, Jade remained pretty much inseparable from her mum. The pair shared manicures, appointments at the hairdressers and meals in fancy restaurants as well as long talks into the night at home. Mum and daughter had got so used to supporting each other over the years that the *Big Brother* series was easily the longest they had been apart since the bleak days of Jackiey's hospitalisation, more than a decade earlier. Jade's mum actually had such a massive asthma attack after watching her daughter first go into the *Big Brother* house that she had to be taken to hospital for emergency treatment. Jackiey said the attack began when she realised just how hard it was going to be for her to live without her daughter for so many weeks. Meanwhile, Jade herself had been the only one of the female housemates to take a photo of her mum into the house with her, and said that catching up with family and old friends was the highlight of her release from the *Big Brother* compound – ahead even of seeing the recorded message from Johnny Depp and meeting other celebrities such as Graham Norton.

In the years ahead it would also be apparent that Jade's old friends were still very much part of her life. To this day she still talks about starting her longed-for beauty business with some of them, if her media career ever stalls, and many faces from her childhood still join her on holidays and gather round for special occasions such as birthdays.

But back in 2002 there was one other person from Jade's past who was casting a long and more difficult shadow: her estranged father, Andy, who was serving a four-year sentence in jail.

Sadly, Andy seemed happy to cash in on his daughter's new-found fame and at one stage he even tried to paint himself as the innocent victim of what he saw as her out-of-control sexuality. 'When she was with PJ every cell door in the jail was banging in time. It was twice the noise they made when England scored in the World Cup,' he said self-centredly, claiming his life had been 'made hell' in prison by Jade's behaviour. At this stage he was in Bedford Prison, having been jailed for robbery, deception and theft.

Three months later, however, he had been moved to a different prison in Nottingham and Jade decided she should visit him in person to try and sort out their differences, put the past behind them and repair their fractured family.

It was never going to be an easy visit, as she and her father were little more than strangers after so many years apart. Jade said little to her driver on the two-hour drive up to the prison before sitting quietly in the car until the official visiting hours began. Strangely enough, walking into the prison to find the visiting hall itself was like a bleak reminder of her first entrance into the *Big Brother* house. There was the same high security, the same body searches and the same barbed-wire fences. But this was no television game show; no music was playing and there were no smiling faces in any crowd. This was real life, not reality TV. And despite all the other prison visits Jade had carried out to see her dad as a child and as a teenager, this one was as hard as anything else she had ever done.

Tense and nervous, the pair hugged after saying their first, uncomfortably formal hellos in the prison's visiting area. Prisoner visits lasted just 40 minutes on that occasion – not enough time to have a really important conversation, but enough time to at least try and say what needed to be said. Jade bought her dad a chocolate bar and a cup of tea from the canteen and started off trying to tell him all about her life inside and outside the *Big Brother* house. She told him about her new personal trainer and her weight loss, about her new home and about some of the celebrity events she was lucky enough to attend, such as the National TV Awards, where she had ended up on stage helping to collect an award for *Big Brother*. She told him about the *Coronation Street* stars she had met and had had a laugh with at the ceremony, and about how she had joked about trying to get an acting role as the Rovers Return's loud new cockney barmaid – an ambition she holds to this day.

Worried about other people's feelings, as usual, Jade even started to cry and apologised to Andy for not having visited him sooner, even though he had effectively walked out on her when she was two and had subsequently visited her so few times during her long, troubled childhood.

But Andy, to his credit, then told Jade the one thing that meant the most to her. That he was proud of her and of everything she had achieved. It was the kind of confidence boost and reassurance Jade could have done with years ago. But it was better late than never and Jade says it is a sentiment she will never forget.

'It was really lovely to see her and she is looking great,' said prisoner number DN9109 when the short visit was over and a tearful and subdued Jade was being driven back down south to her home. 'Everyone dismissed Jade as being thick and loud but she seems to be doing really well. She's now mixing with a lot of stars but she won't let it go to her head.'

Andy was also starting to see the impact his own lifestyle had had on his daughter. 'I know only too well that I

The still unknown Jade gets ready to meet her housemates.

Free at last!

Top: Jade – about to burst out of her favourite dress as Davina McCall leads her out of the Big Brother house.

Above: Davina takes charge as Jade faces the public.

Top: Jade and series winner Kate Lawler at a Big Brother book launch.

Above: Living the high life – a glamorous Jade kisses fellow housemate Alex Sibley at a celebrity party in 2002.

Jade does her bit to raise awareness of Cancer Research UK – one of the many charities she has signed up to support.

Top: A passionate kiss for Jeff Brazier when the couple were still very much in love.
Above: Jeff and Jade hit the town in 2003.

Top: Jade can still laugh with her 'celebrity stalker' Avid Merrion.

Above: Posing with fellow celebrity Jordan – before Jade had a boob job of her own.

Top: Jade having fun with Patsy Palmer and their children.

Above: Proud dad Jeff and little Bobby do their bit for the Woodland Trust charity appeal.

Top: Jade has a second go at passing her driving test – after very publicly failing on Celebrity Driving School.

Above: Having successfully passed, Jade takes her new Merc for a spin. But unfortunately ends up giving it a prang!

haven't been the best father to Jade,' he said. 'But I'm determined to be there now, whenever she needs me.' Other visitors to the Nottingham prison that day said that, despite the obvious tension, father and daughter did seem to have some kind of bond. And they said Jade had behaved impeccably. 'When Jade first came into the waiting area everyone was open-mouthed,' said a fellow visitor. 'Not all the inmates know her dad is here. But Jade didn't act the star, she obviously wanted to be treated the same as everyone else. When she first got to the prison a few inmates asked her for an autograph. She was fine about it and everybody really liked and respected her.'

When the prison visit took place, in October 2002, Andy had been hoping to be given a release date – and was determined to go straight and do the best he could for his suddenly successful daughter.

Sadly, things didn't quite work out that way. Andy was indeed freed the following summer, but he was far from the caring dad Jade had dreamed he would turn into. No one knows if he called the papers and magazines first, or if they contacted him and made him offers he was in no position to refuse. But, however it began, Andy decided to take their money and do their bidding. 'The whole *Big Brother* experience has fixed up the family. It's a godsend,' he had said optimistically to a different reporter who had tracked him down between prisons the previous year. And he was ready to cash in on it again.

So Jade woke up one morning in the summer of 2003 to read a series of lurid articles based on interviews given by her estranged father. What was worse was the fact that many of the stories were illustrated with private family photographs he had happily supplied to the reporters.

Not surprisingly, Jade was devastated. 'I don't think I can ever heal the rift between me and my father,' she said tearfully, unable to believe that he could break his promises and betray her so easily and so fast. 'I didn't tell my mum but I gave him money when he came out of prison and I tried to help him. But he stabbed me in the back by selling pictures of me to the papers. He let me down and I've now disowned him. It's hard enough keeping my private life private without him invading it.'

In the final irony Jade pointed out that Andy was in fact the very last person who could claim to know any of her secrets in the first place. 'He doesn't know about my life and he's never been any part of it,' she said. 'My mum Jackiey's my best friend. She's always been both a mum and a dad to me.' Jackiey, fortunately, was keeping mum in every sense of the word. She was supporting her daughter to the end, even though her former lover Andy was still hoping he could be given another chance.

A series of tense telephone conversations took place between him, Jackiey and Andy was hoping for a full reconciliation with his family. As it turned out, this reconciliation was going to have to take place back inside a jail, just like the last time. After missing a probation appointment in the autumn, Andy was sent back to prison to serve the remaining portion of his previous jail term. He had been free for just three short months.

Sorry for himself to the end, Andy spoke to the papers from his new cell in Devon. 'My life was coming together and this happens,' he said. 'The best thing was that my daughter was beginning to trust me again – and that was giving me the strength to carry on. Now I don't know what I'm going to do.' Yet Jade knew what she was going to do. She was going to move on – and would never speak about the subject again.

Unfortunately, while that chapter of her life was closing, another few unsavoury pages were being turned elsewhere. The wider Goody family was as troubled as it had ever been and Jade's extraordinary family nightmare was to continue.

Shortly after Andy had been sent back to prison, Jade's equally estranged grandmother was arrested for stealing baby clothes from the Woolworths near her home in Stoke Newington, North London. It was just the latest arrest in a career of shop thefts going back 27 years – and the 65-year-old grandmother admitted she had been high on crack cocaine when she was caught.

'I'm very sorry if I have brought shame on Jade. I was so proud of her when she appeared on television,' said Jacqueline, trying to make amends to her estranged granddaughter. But she then made matters worse by forgetting about and failing to turn up for sentencing at Redbridge magistrates' court, triggering the *Daily Star* to run a massive story under the headline, 'Jade's gran on the run – cops hunt for court bunk OAP.'

When a new court date was set, Jade's grandmother tried to get her solicitor to explain her actions. 'My client had developed an addiction to crack, which has been difficult to break,' her lawyer Paul Mason told the court before sentencing. 'She expresses a desire to give up.'

But District Judge Alison Rose was unconvinced. 'You have been offered chances in the community with help from psychiatrists, none of which you have complied with. The only thing I can do is to send you to prison for a total of six months,' she said.

When the sentence had been handed out, Jade tried once more to put the various black sheep of her troubled family out of her mind. 'I don't even call her my nan and I've never had anything to do with her, or that side of my family,' she said of her jailbird grandmother before trying once more to close this chapter for good as well.

Mercifully, Jade could rely on some firm friends from her past to fight her corner whenever times were tough. Old pal Clem Green was ready to defend her when *Big Brother* winner Kate Lawler allegedly grabbed the PA system in a local pub and told shocked drinkers how much she hated Jade and wanted to fight her. 'For the most part I think Jade will just laugh this off and try and be adult about it,' said Clem at the time. 'But Kate should be very careful about this fight, if she knows what's good for her. She obviously thinks it won't really happen and is just trying to make herself look big. But if Jade bumps into her after this, I think she would be like: "OK then, let's do it." And then Kate would be in real trouble. There would only be one winner and it certainly wouldn't be Kate. Jade would slaughter her.'

In the earliest days after *Big Brother* ended, other people far from the public eye were also lining up to support the embattled Jade. Bermondsey was always ready to protect its own.

'Jade fits in round here, she's really well liked,' said neighbour Nickola Evans, who ran a hairdressing salon near Jade's mum's house and was determined to show that Jade would always be welcome to come back to her old haunts. 'She'll be cheered up and down the high street here. She's just up for a laugh, Jade is.'

But behind the scenes Jade was actually getting serious. She had absolutely no idea if her sudden fame would last, or if she would suddenly be plunged back into obscurity when a new tabloid sensation hit the scene. But if this was her one chance at a new life in the media, she was determined to try and grasp it. After a shaky start on Graham Norton's chat shows and other live interview shows, she realised that she quite liked performing in front of the cameras. Once she got over her nerves, answering questions and chatting was actually fun. But she knew that she couldn't stay a chat-show guest for ever. If she was going to get anywhere, she would have to learn to present a show, which would involve getting to grips with the fact that her reading skills were so poor – another of her most personal demons.

The issue of Jade's literacy – or lack of it – had raised its head many times in the *Big Brother* house, especially when she had been picked to read out instructions to fellow housemates. And unless she tackled it soon then reading a script and following an autocue was going to be pretty difficult.

'Jade can't do her own television programme until she can read properly,' admitted mum Jackiey. 'But she's not embarrassed about this any more and she's now got a tutor for reading and spelling.' Neither of them knew if the investment would be worthwhile. But Jade was on a mission of self-improvement in the second half of 2002. 'I've just got to buck my ideas up when I get out,' she had said in the final days of *Big Brother*. Now she was being as good as her word and wanted some peace and quiet while she buckled down to her new lessons.

Sad to say, despite all their best intentions, some friends inadvertently increased the pressures on Jade as she tried to cope with life in the spotlight. A group of old friends went with her to a wild party night at the flash Emporium nightclub near London's Regents Street. Now called Tantra, the club has VIP areas, mirrored ceilings and the world's largest under-lit glass dance floor. It is a favourite with celebrities, and the paparazzi will often wait outside in the hope of seeing a famous face. They were there when Jade and her friends arrived that November night. 'My friend's boyfriend stuck his coat over my head, really as a joke,' Jade said, without thinking any more of it. But while Jade was having fun in the club – dancing with, among other people, Page Three girl and porn star Linsey Dawn McKenzie – newspaper executives were plotting yet another attack on the single 21-year-old.

The following morning they printed the pictures of Jade under her pal's coat and laid into her for supposedly acting like a diva and overestimating her own importance. While poring over the coverage with her friends to try and work out what on earth she had done wrong, Jade realised that, like many celebrities, she was effectively damned if she did, and damned if she didn't. If she was happy to stand around and be snapped by photographers outside a club, she was called a desperate wannabe who is addicted to fame. If she tried to make a discreet entrance and exit, she was accused of snubbing her fans – a prima donna 'who seems unaware that a few months ago she was nothing', as the *Daily Star* pointed out cruelly on another occasion when Jade asked photographers to leave her friends in peace during a birthday celebration.

But while Jade was able to laugh at all these mixed messages from the media, could she laugh about the less kindly responses of some of her former *Big Brother* housemates? 'On a show like *Big Brother* you don't really make friends because there is so much bitching going on,' she admitted six months after leaving the house.

Yet PJ was happy to bury the hatchet with the girl he had publicly humiliated after their night of supposed passion. 'I'm sorry about how I treated her and how I tried to ignore her after the incident,' he said. 'I haven't been a gentleman where she is concerned but now I would love to take her out for lunch or dinner and say sorry, and stay in touch.'

Meanwhile, Alex – who had his own very public ups and downs with Jade in the *Big Brother* house – was also a valued confidante back in the real world. The pair spoke on the phone frequently to help each other through the media minefield they had found themselves in. Cambridge-based Spencer also stayed in touch, though Jade's famously sketchy understandings of where exactly Cambridge was meant visits were few and far between.

However, some other former contestants would remain ready to twist the knife in Jade's back many years after they had all left the Elstree compound. Jade was thrilled to go out on the town and be photographed in early 2004 with her new slim figure and glamorous new look, for instance. Style writers in the papers applauded – one even compared the former Bermondsey bruiser to the ultra-glam Elizabeth Hurley. But not everyone was impressed.

'All she has done is dye her hair from blonde to brunette. It's not difficult. She may dress a bit better but she's still got the same gob on her,' Kate was quoted as saying, possibly smarting from the news that her own job as a presenter on Channel 4's troubled breakfast show *RI:SE* had just ended.

Old friends such as Clem Green say Jade does sometimes cry in private when she reads the worst stories and criticisms about herself. But in public she has always managed to keep her head held high.

'There has been a lot of nastiness about me,' she told *OK!* magazine in an exclusive interview when asked if she was hurt by all the false and malicious stories about her. 'I don't need all that. I've been through the stage of reading all those stories saying I'm fat and I'm ugly. Although I'm a strong person, it is hard to deal with. It's awkward, you overcome one obstacle and then there is another in your way.'

And, unfortunately, as Jade's career began to gather momentum, a whole lot more obstacles were already being laid out in front of her. Some of them were to be work-based. Others would stand between her and the stable relationship and family life that she craved. And some, a few years hence, would narrowly threaten her life.

chapter 8

It's Jade
Versus Geri

Splitting her favourite pair of white French Connection cords on Day 57 in the Big Brother house had been a big wake-up call for Jade. 'I thought I would have a giggle and see how far I could get them up – then I ripped them all the way down the side,' she said to a laughing Alex and Tim. 'Then I put my green skirt on and I could feel myself hanging out of it. Then I put another jean skirt on – because they are all a size 12, which I was when I came into the house – and it didn't fit me. So I put this white skirt on and it wouldn't go past my bum. I've gone up a whole dress size – at least.'

From that moment on, Jade was constantly looking at her ever-growing body in the mirror and what she called her 'kebab belly' soon entered the vocabulary of the country. 'I'll never be a sex symbol with my belly,' she said ruefully while getting changed for a dip in the house hot tub one evening.

The nine-week series had certainly taken its toll on the 21-year-old chocoholic. 'I've always been a big girl, but never this big. I've got to sort this out,' she said to Kate, who remained stubbornly stick-thin for the whole show. 'I'm not going to go shopping till I lose weight. And if I go out with my mates now I won't be able to fit in any of their cars. They'll have to strap me on to the roof.'

Once outside the house, Jade wasn't able to forget her heavyweight new image either. From her eviction evening onwards she would be shown clip after unflattering clip of her body and the way she tried to cover it up. 'By the end of *Big Brother* I couldn't fit into any of the clothes I had taken into the house with me 10 weeks before,' she said, trying to explain her bizarre but limited fashion ensembles in the show's last few days. 'The only thing I could get on was my trackie bottoms and bikinis with my belly hanging out over them. I was mortified.'

The reason for the transformation was simple. 'Sometimes there wasn't a lot to do apart from sit around and eat,' she said. 'That isn't something I would normally do, as I am always on the go. The fridge was always full of food and chocolate, and I couldn't help myself. I knew I was putting on weight but I didn't realise how much until the end. One day I even ate two family-size Galaxy bars in 10 minutes.' The drinking didn't help either. This series of *Big Brother* turned out to be one of the booziest of all the shows and Jade probably went through more than her fair share of the wine on offer – piling on a lot more pounds in the process.

For some reason the British public proved to dislike the

few positive influences in the house that could have taught Jade how to keep in shape. Fitness fan Lynne and female bodybuilder Adele were both voted out, and left to her own devices Jade found it hard to get inspired to exercise. She was certainly no fan of traditional weight-loss strategies. Her three minutes on the house running machine was subsequently voted one of the top ten funniest scenes in the whole history of *Big Brother*. 'I'm going to be a fit bird now,' she had yelled, before launching herself at the machine, going bright red, gasping for air and worrying that her bouncing boobs might give her a black eye as they threatened to burst out of her tightly buttoned top.

'It's lucky there's no scales in here,' she said, and, after a few more abortive attempts to run off a few pounds on the house stairwell, Jade began spending more and more time in bed, on the sofa and in a deckchair. Eating and drinking pretty much every waking hour.

So how did she feel when she came out of the house and realised just how obsessed people had become about what she had been eating and how much she weighed? 'I thought it was all a bit mad but I laughed it off because I didn't think that I was obese. I've always been a bit big but there are far bigger people out there than me. And that coverage about me was hurtful to half the people in the country who are a bit big and read the papers. They must think like, Oh my God, if they think she's big, I must be obese, and things like that. But there's nothing wrong with being a size 16 or whatever. It was only a problem for me because I had been a size 10 and went up to a very tight size 14 in such a short time period, so I wanted to go back down again. People should only try to lose weight when they want to lose it for themselves and not because of anybody else.'

Having had friends who had almost become ill worrying about their weight, Jade was particularly sensitive about the subject. 'Anorexia is a terrible illness and I knew there would be lots of teenage girls watching the show so I didn't want them getting the idea that they should be going on a diet too. That's why I used to get annoyed with some of the other housemates who used to go on about being fat when they were really skinny.'

Outside the *Big Brother* house, Jade realised she didn't just want to lose a bit of her new weight so she could squeeze back into her old clothes, she wanted to get fit as well. Gone were the days when she just sat on a stool in a dental surgery all day. Her new life had a surprisingly tough schedule and she needed to build up her stamina to keep up. Appearing on a television chat show, speaking to a journalist or having some publicity photos taken may not seem the toughest physical challenges in the world. But when they all need to take place on the same day, in very different parts of London, you need a lot of energy to keep up.

Her first try at fitness came courtesy of the *Sun*, which put her in touch with top personal trainer Jamie Stone. Jamie then took charge of her exercise regime at the exclusive Oasis gym in Marlow, Buckinghamshire. 'She isn't fat at all,' he said gallantly after measuring his nervous new charge. 'She just needs to lose a few pounds and tone up a bit. If she did a decent hour-long workout three times a week, she would see good results in four weeks.'

But it looked as if traditional hour-long workouts weren't likely to work for Jade. 'Oh my God, this is some sort of torture machine,' she yelled as she tried to lift the first set of weights Jamie set up for her. Resistance machines got a similar thumbs down as Jade got in turns confused, bored and tired by the way they all worked.

So, with gyms and exercise bikes out of the question, Jade decided to go back to what had always worked for her in the past. She decided to try dancing her way thin instead. She danced at home whenever she had a free moment – normally to music, but sometimes in silence or accompanied by her own versions of the latest hits. She danced in the living room, the bedroom, the kitchen and in front of the bathroom mirror. She did a few steps when she was bored, waiting in corridors for meetings to start, or immediately after filming an interview show while she waited to be taken to the hospitality room to wind down. And as the weeks passed she realised it was working. The pounds finally fell off her, she went down the two dress sizes she had been aiming for and felt more toned and muscular than she had ever done before. A couple of magazine cover shots showed just how much her face and her figure changed. And suddenly everyone wanted to talk about it.

'It's great – people have actually been saying to me, "You look fantastic" and "How did you do it?" I love it!' she said when the last few pounds had finally fallen away. 'Complete strangers have been coming up to me in Tesco and telling me I look stunning. I've had a few guys asking me to marry them and the other night at a club these two male models were saying, "Come home with us." I was like, "Oh my God, no!" and I couldn't believe it,' Jade said, revelling in the compliments after so much criticism and abuse in the recent past. And there was an even bigger surprise to come.

'I was in a cab the other day and the taxi driver said he had just read a magazine article that had listed me as one of the top celebrity bodies in the world! I said he must be joking but ever since other people have been ringing up and congratulating me. Now I've seen the article myself I have to admit I'm actually quite chuffed.' And so she should have been. More than 10,000 people had voted in the international poll for *Celebrity Bodies* magazine. They had put established stars Kylie Minogue, Halle Berry and Jennifer Lopez in the top three positions; and, while Jade was a long way behind at 50th, she was still ranked well ahead of her South-London neighbour and supermodel Naomi Campbell, and just one place below super-fit tennis babe Anna Kournkova.

Even though Jade and her friends laughed at the list, she soon realised it wasn't just male models and taxi drivers who were interested in her new look and the way she had made it happen. Video producers were also on the phone to Jade's management company because they reckoned the public would love to know more about what she had been doing and to watch her routines first-hand.

Producing a fitness video is a common and sometimes lucrative move for female celebrities. But in the autumn of 2002 Jade was uncertain if she should go ahead with one. For a start, she wasn't sure she could yet claim to be a celebrity. She wasn't convinced that anyone would really be interested in her routines. And she wasn't confident enough in her ability as a dancer.

The professionals thought differently, however. Star choreographer Kevin Adams, the chief dance coach on the first series of BBC One's *Fame Academy* who has also worked with Cher, Mariah Carey and Boyzone, was certain that Jade had what it would take to get through the dance routines. And video producers and marketing managers were convinced that the public would prefer to find out how someone like Jade had got in shape, rather than an alternative celebrity who looked as if she hadn't eaten more than a few lettuce leaves in her whole life.

Jade herself realised that the job would also give her some valuable extra experience in front of the cameras – vital if she was ever to achieve her goal of a full-time career in the media. So, after many last-minute doubts, she agreed to go ahead. When the contracts had been signed, Kevin and his assistant Lisa Jones got down to business with Jade. The two experts took a look at their new star's existing routines, found out what her strengths and weaknesses were, and helped create some new moves for her to try. Kevin and Lisa also found her four handsome male dancers to practise with. Jade ultimately built up an obvious rapport with the foursome and they were brought along to dance with her when the video was finally produced less than six weeks later.

'Jade has had a lot to do but she has worked really hard and has done really well,' said Lisa on day one of the video shoot. 'She's great now.' And Jade was the first to admit it hadn't been an easy journey for any of them. 'When I started doing the video I was as stiff as a carrot and Lisa had to help me find a bit of rhythm,' said Jade, over the moon at her achievements when filming finally began. 'I've got four dancers and I teach them how to do all these dance routines. I'm excited, but nervous as well. I'm doing things I never thought I could do.' And she was going to do them in typical style.

'Don't forget to smile, it's a happy workout, remember,' yelled out video director Steve Kemsley just before the cameras started rolling. But Jade, of all people, hardly needed reminding about that.

Her introduction and chatter was a world away from the standard worthy commentaries on similar productions. 'Don't panic if you feel knackered and need to stop. Just keep moving on the spot and carry on when you get your breath back,' she said in typically direct fashion when introducing the routines. Her signature comment, 'OK, bellies in everyone and off we go,' was equally unique in a fitness world that frequently took itself far too seriously.

With Jade in charge the whole tone of this video was relaxed, irreverent and fun. 'If you can't get the dance moves right straight away, that's fine. The more you do it, the easier it will get,' Jade said at the start. And from then on she laughed, squealed, clapped her hands, called out to her dancers, made faces at the camera and acted like, well, Jade. 'Hey, we ain't finished yet,' she shouted out at one of her dancers at one point when he looked as if he was flagging and got temporarily out of step. It was all what makes Jade seem so human. And it turned out to be what made Jade's video sell by the bucket-load.

From the start Jade had been entirely realistic in the way she presented herself and her fitness routines. 'I'm just like every other woman,' she admitted when promoting the tape. 'I'm not stick-thin and I have to work hard to keep in shape.' Crazy celebrity diets were also a waste of time, according to Jade, because the best way to lose weight was to keep things simple, be more realistic about the temptations you face and what you are likely to achieve. 'I've just been eating really healthily and cutting out bread, chocolate and takeaways. But I won't starve myself of something. I think if you fancy something you can treat yourself every now and then. That's always allowed.'

On the exercise front Jade realised that dancing worked because you don't need any equipment and can do it anywhere. The other fun thing was the acknowledgement that you don't actually need to be that good a dancer. You just need enthusiasm, energy, commitment and a sense of humour – four things that Jade had in massive quantities.

It all meant that the tape was actually a mass of contradictions. At some points Jade and her choreographers had clearly got into the Zone and she looked as polished and professional as any pop star or West End performer. But at other times it all fell apart a little – and Jade burst out laughing as she tried to get back in sync.

Filming the actual dance routines had turned into a lot of fun. While the 12-person crew of set builders, cameramen, sound engineers, stylists and make-up staff watched from the wings, Jade and her boys danced to a series of up-tempo tracks, recording a warm-up, a main set of routines and a five-minute cool-down session.

Occasional retakes and technical problems slowed their progress and Jade changed clothes several times before deciding which outfits would work best for the production. She admitted later that she had loved being the star of the show and she was convinced that viewers at home would enjoy following the routines.

But with the fun part of the job done, Jade faced what turned out to be a slightly bigger challenge: recording the tape's short introduction. At this early stage in her career Jade was happy to admit that she wasn't entirely relaxed when she was placed squarely in front of a camera. Being filmed 24 hours a day in the *Big Brother* house had been fine because you could pretty much forget about the cameras, and weren't always sure exactly where they were, anyway. Talking on chat shows was also less stressful than it might have been because you can focus entirely on the person asking you questions and pretend that the cameras don't exist.

Doing a voice-over direct to camera is a different matter, however. The camera is, of course, right in front of you. And it takes a long time to get as confident about talking directly into it as the likes of Davina McCall and Dermot O'Leary. 'It sounds ridiculous but you really do have to imagine that this big mechanical object in front of you is actually a living human being,' says media trainer Frances Wright, who tells the bosses of some of Britain's biggest companies how they can look relaxed and confident on camera. 'You need to imagine it as a friend of yours, someone you want to talk to, someone whose reactions you care about. It has to be your focus all the time, even when you think things are going wrong. You will notice that the very best television presenters never look away from the cameras and always give the impression that there is no one else in the room with them.'

Yet Jade hadn't quite got this message when the time came to record her brief 'Dance Workout' introduction. She had struggled with the same thing in the pre-publicity for *Big Brother* when the housemates all had to sit still in front of the camera for a few moments without saying a word. None of the other housemates had a problem. But Jade lasted less than 10 seconds before bursting out with laughter and apologising profusely.

In the converted warehouse where the video shoot was taking place, in the autumn of 2002, her nerves were starting to show again. After just a few words her eyes would dart away from the camera towards the director, choreographer or any other friendly face for confirmation that she was doing OK. So they had to shoot the scene again and again until she got the confidence to give the camera her full attention.

It was embarrassing stuff. But Jade was determined to learn from incidents like these rather than to feel ashamed of them. She wanted to store up these lessons to ensure she would get better in front of the cameras as time went on. That way, if there was ever to be a follow-up fitness video, she would be ready for it.

But when director Steve Kemsley called a wrap on that first tape, a sequel was the last thing on anyone's minds. The big gamble was whether a public more used to serious and sometimes unrealistic routines from fitness professionals would warm to Jade's entirely honest display in this tape. There was a real worry that it might not even sell enough to cover its costs.

The video and DVD, 'Jade's Dance Workout', hit the shops in time for the Christmas market in late 2002. It was in good company. Fellow *Big Brother* contestant Kate Lawler, forever referred to as the show's fit, pretty star, had made a fitness video based on her well-publicised love of kick-boxing. It was released on exactly the same day as Jade's tape. And at first glance Kate's looked to be the more obvious best-seller because she had spent so much time practising her fitness routines in the *Big Brother* house and had a great body to start with.

Meanwhile, other more established entertainment and fitness names were fighting for the nation's attention. *Coronation Street* beauty and tabloid darling Tracy Shaw had a 'Salsacise' video out, based on the suddenly popular Latin dance craze. Fellow *Corrie* star Jennifer James was also in the market with a video alongside *EastEnder* Lucy Benjamin. The model and lad's mag favourite Nell McAndrew had also released the latest in her long series of best-selling fitness and exercise tapes.

Last into battle was Jade's biggest rival of all – the publicity-aware former Spice Girl Geri Halliwell, who had jumped on the yoga bandwagon with an Eastern-influenced tape she credited with having created her own amazing new look.

So-called experts in the media were called in to give their verdicts on the various offerings. In the *Daily Mail* Carolan Brown, billed as a former personal trainer to Princess

Diana, was typically harsh. She gave 'Jade's Dance Workout' the lowest score of all the tapes she reviewed – a grim 0/10 to be exact. But, to be fair to Carolan, she wasn't much more generous to Kate, who scored just 2/10. Geri, Patsy Palmer and Cindy Crawford all got awarded 5/10, while Tracy Shaw got 7/10, and GMTV newsreader and television presenter Penny Smith's 'Yoga Masterclass' was judged the best of the bunch with 9/10.

The British public, however, had other ideas. The line on the cover of Jade's video asked one simple question: 'How did she get to look so good?' And it seemed that thousands of women were more than happy to pay up to £17.99 to find out. Against all the odds Jade's video and DVD immediately topped the sales charts at both Woolworths and HMV – where she enjoyed more than double the sales of Kate Lawler. And, while she wasn't the type of person to gloat, Jade had to admit she was pleased.

'For me it's never been a competition or a battle with Kate. I did something I enjoyed doing and I wanted to share it with everybody else. And I've learned something out of it. So it's never really been a competition, but it is nice that when Kate thought that it was a battle and said, "Let the battle begin," that I've come out on top.'

Jade even outsold the legendary exercise and diet queen Rosemary Conley in December 2002 – and when the figures were finally added up, it turned out that, from among the 22 new health and fitness titles available that month, in the crucial pre-Christmas period, Jade had easily hit the number-one spot.

As for the much-hyped battle between Jade and Geri? Jade

won by a mile. She ended up with the best-selling fitness video of 2002 – earning her a minimum of £80,000 in just three months. Jade was also enjoying some seriously flattering attention about her new look – much of which surprised her so much, she ended up lost for words. 'Jade, do you see yourself as a sex symbol now?' one journalist asked her after reviewing Jade's latest portfolio of photographs.

Jade laughed in disbelief and couldn't bring herself to reply. 'At one point I was being called a pig, so the fact that you would even ask me a question like that is quite a turnaround,' was all she could think of to say. Unluckily, despite all the early compliments and attention, Jade didn't enjoy an entirely easy ride in the fitness stakes and many of the people who bought the tape were somewhat underwhelmed by it.

The official review of her video on Internet retailer Amazon was scathing, for instance. 'Jade neither looks nor acts the dance part. With four hunky guys strutting their fab, professional dance bodies, unfortunately Jade is shown up for what she is: inept,' it proclaimed. Other reviewers had mixed opinions. 'The dances get boring and Jade can't really dance,' said one shopper from Bristol. 'But the video is fun and Jade goes wrong sometimes so that's funny.'

The production itself wasn't well judged either. 'It all seems quite cheap and hastily put together,' said one reviewer, while another suggested that the best thing to do is to follow the male backing dancers rather than Jade. 'Her comments and calling can get seriously annoying,' she concluded. However, full-time fitness professionals gave Jade a qualified thumbs up.

Personal trainer Mia Sanchez, who has taught in many of London's most exclusive private health clubs and now works for a variety of well-known individual and corporate names, says that, despite some criticism, Jade was in fact the ideal person to front an exercise tape. 'I know from my own experience and from all my clients that there is nothing so disheartening as being taught fitness or dance moves by someone with a perfect body or by someone who is so polished and slick that they look as if they are from another planet. Real, ordinary women tend to respond better when they are being shown things by other real, ordinary women. If you are trying to follow a routine in your own home you don't want to end up feeling foolish because you keep getting things wrong, so it is comforting that Jade clearly struggles a bit sometimes as well. But, that said, you do need to feel sure that your instructor is properly qualified for the job and Jade doesn't always project enough credibility on this front.'

Yet Sanchez still believes Jade was right to make the tape. 'By doing a fitness video Jade was opening herself up for some more cruel criticism of her body and a repeat of the abuse she suffered on *Big Brother*, so she deserves some credit for accepting the challenge,' she says.

Still, the media found it impossible to pay Jade any compliments without attaching a few cruel barbs. The *Daily Mail* put Jade alongside Gwyneth Paltrow on the 'Going Up' side of its style barometer in January 2003, for example. She got a positive ranking because her fitness video was 'selling like hot cakes' said the paper. But it couldn't leave it like that. 'The video was one of the nation's favourite joke presents at Christmas,' the reporter claimed, sticking in the knife as always.

As far as Jade was concerned, it was all just water off a duck's back. She could laugh along with her friends at those sort of comments because she had done more than just earn money, prestige and a better figure from her fitness video. It turned out that the personal trainer she had called up for advice about losing weight immediately after leaving the *Big Brother* house had a flatmate. He was a former Leyton Orient footballer and was now working as a part-time model and a television presenter. His name was Jeff Brazier, and Jade was about to fall head over heels in love with him.

chapter 9

Escape to...
Essex

On the morning after the 1997 General Election, Cherie Blair
famously opened her front door wearing just her nightdress –
and found unflattering pictures of herself all over the front
pages the next day. So perhaps Jeff Brazier should have
thought a little harder about his appearance before answering
the bell at his Harlow home the morning after the night before
with Jade.

Photographers first snapped the former builder and
footballer when he appeared at the door out of breath
and only wearing a towel. Hours later, after the couple
had gone for a brief shopping trip, the reporters
knocked once again. And this time Jeff appeared in front
of them startled and wearing only a pair of white
football shorts.

'Busty *Big Brother* star Jade Goody has a new love – and
he's as keen as her to get his kit off,' screamed the papers

the next day, referring to Jade's infamous drunken strip in the *Big Brother* house.

Most of the reporters got Jeff's name wrong, however. In early reports he was widely referred to as 'Jeff Adams', a reference to Jade's personal trainer Kevin Adams, who owned the house where all three of them were staying. But after a while Jeff Brazier's real name was going to get heard a whole lot more. And at first he was to prove to be quite a gentleman.

'Jade is a lovely girl, the nicest of the *Big Brother* bunch and she comes across even better in real life,' he said. 'I used to throw things at the telly when I first saw her on the show but by the end of the series, like everyone else, I really liked her and felt sorry for her. I felt I wanted to know what she was really like. I knew she would be a laugh but I never expected us to get on as well as we did when we first met. Jade was never the housemate I would have voted for at first, but when you meet her in person you see a different side, and that's the side I liked.'

At this point Jeff had just appeared in the Channel 4 reality show *Shipwrecked* and was finding his own way through the lower levels of the media jungle. He was hoping to become a full-time television presenter and was sharing a house with old pal Kevin Adams, the personal trainer who had transformed Jade's body after *Big Brother* and got her in shape for her first fitness video. Jade herself had moved in a few months earlier to make sure she stayed on track when following his new fitness routines. And Jeff was quick to say that his old friend Kevin had done a fantastic job. 'Jade's looking great now, really toned. All the exercise has paid off,' he told the press in his towel that first morning.

For her part, Jade had liked the look of Jeff from the first moment Kevin had shown her a picture of him and suggested a date. But the couple took things slowly. It was complicated being housemates as well as potential partners and neither was sure of the right way forward. 'There wasn't any sexual attraction at first but I really liked Jade and cared about her,' says Jeff, who at 23 was two years older than Jade. 'We used to muck about together, cuddling and things. It was a gradual thing.'

In fact, romance had actually dawned in the Lake District, a month before the press found out about their relationship in the late autumn of 2002. 'Me, Jeff, Kevin and his girlfriend Helen went away on a walking trip,' says Jade. 'I'm such a girlie and I hate getting dirty but we had a real laugh. Jeff and me were sharing a room and there was only one bed. We were friends and I wanted to know if I was something more to him. He's totally different to anyone else I've ever been out with and he's lovely.'

'It just happened,' says Jeff when he too thinks back to that weekend in the Lake District. 'By then there was so much between us and the rest seemed like fate. I've never been happier.' What mattered most to Jade at this stage in her life was having some security and stability away from the limelight. Always insecure, she needed a reassuring, calming and supportive other half. She needed someone who she felt would be on her side, no matter what. And someone who, unlike her *Big Brother* housemates, would include her in everything and help her forget a childhood spent out of step with normal family life.

That someone really did look like it could be Jeff. Friends said he was a steady, reliable rock of a man. He could be quiet, he listened to others, tried to understand them and always aimed to avoid conflict. And as a fellow television performer he could appreciate what Jade was going through and all the challenges she had ahead of her.

It looked like a perfect match – but, in typical Jade Goody fashion, the couple couldn't have a calm, slow-burning relationship. Crisis number one came just a matter of weeks after they had first officially started dating. Jade had been trying to fix the telephone intercom system at the home she had moved to in Thurrock, Essex. She used a pair of scissors to prise out two live wires and then slipped as she tried to push them back into the socket. In one awful moment she fell against the scissors, piercing her right eye and leaving her screaming in pain.

'The pain was excruciating and it was even more frightening to be covered in blood,' says a friend whom Jade spoke to in hospital 'She remembers feeling faint and falling to the floor, terrified that she had permanently damaged her eye.' Jeff was the first person Jade called when she struggled to find her mobile phone.

He dashed to her home and found her, still bleeding, on the living-room floor. Jeff drove her to their local hospital, where doctors gave her emergency treatment before she was referred to the world-famous Moorfields Eye Hospital in London. Specialists there said they could save her eye – though she had to wear an eyepatch for days before their treatment even began to take effect. It had been a terrifying few days. But at least the emergency had helped to bring the couple even closer together. Jade had learned one crucial lesson: Jeff was a good man to have around in a crisis. He was supportive, caring, quick-witted and practical – the kind of man she would have liked to have had in her home when she was growing up.

Their relationship was suddenly looking a whole lot stronger. Which was just as well – because it was about to be tested even more.

Jade left Moorfields and tried to get back to normal. She wasn't feeling fantastic, but she put her tiredness down to her extraordinarily punishing new schedule. The tough keep-fit routine she had been on before the filming of her dance video was only one part of her new workload. She was also talking to several television production companies about future shows, continuing with her long line of newspaper and magazine interviews, and having several new sets of photos taken for magazine covers and fashion spreads. In addition she was trying to get to grips with the serious side of her new life, fitting in meetings with everyone from her agents and management company to her new lawyers and financial advisers. On top of that she was attending gruelling rehearsals for her first-ever live stage role. In December she was to be the biggest name in *Snow White and the Seven Dwarfs* at the high-profile Woodville Halls theatre in Kent. The producers were paying her a record amount of money to appear – so she knew she had to deliver a great performance in return. It was stressful stuff for someone who had never been on a professional stage before and had never had any formal theatre training.

With all that to worry about, it was little wonder that

Jade felt exhausted. But when she was honest with herself she had to admit that tiredness, stress and worries had never made her feel this ill before. So could something else be to blame for her sudden loss of energy? Jade desperately hoped not. Her career was just starting to take off and she had only met this wonderful new man a matter of weeks before, so the very last thing she wanted was to be pregnant. 'Could I have been so stupid?' she asked herself. 'Surely I just have a mild virus or I'm suffering from a winter bug,' she hoped.

All the same, when her increasingly tough panto rehearsals were over one day she went into a local chemist to buy a pregnancy test. It took her some time to even pluck up the courage to open the box. Jade was just 21 years old. The daughter of a young single mother herself, she had never even considered following in her mother's footsteps so soon. Jade had always dreamed of getting married before getting pregnant, and she was currently enjoying real freedom for the first time in her life. Was all that about to come to an end?

Jade couldn't wait any longer before finding out. So she tore open the box, followed the instructions and waited, alone and terrified, for the result. When it came, it couldn't have been clearer. The little blue line was exactly where the instructions said it should be. It wasn't a virus, it wasn't a bug, tiredness or stress. Jade was expecting a baby.

'I was on the Pill so I never thought it would happen,' she said. 'But I had terrible pains in my stomach and I could almost feel myself getting bigger. Jeff kept joking that I was having a baby but when I found out I was in total shock. I was crying because it just wasn't planned.' Jeff, however, came up trumps once more. 'I called him and he was so lovely, supportive and positive that I started feeling better immediately,' Jade said. 'We are both so excited.' But even with this good news on the horizon Jade couldn't stop herself from laughing at her own expense. 'It's typical of me that pregnancy has coincided with my fitness video,' she said. 'There's me going on about losing weight and I'm going to be ballooning out all over the place.' And Jade was convinced that she would balloon like the best of them. 'I wish I was going to be neat and perfect like Kate Moss or Sarah Jessica Parker – they looked lovely when they were pregnant,' she said. 'But I think I will end up absolutely huge.'

Jeff, thankfully, didn't care about his girlfriend's figure. He was only 23, and his life and media career were only just beginning as well. But he was determined to look on the bright side – for Jade's sake as well as his own. 'Everything has happened so fast but both of us are still smiling,' he said once they had both adjusted to the news. 'I think Jade will be a fantastic mother. She'll still be dippy but no one will love our baby more. Jade may be mad as a hatter but she's such a sweet and caring girl. I love her bump and keep feeling her tummy, stroking the baby.'

Neither Jade nor Jeff was born with a silver spoon in their mouth. Jeff's childhood was happy and although Jade's childhood was in many ways difficult, she has always managed to look back on it fondly. 'We both had hard upbringings but we were both happy kids,' said Jade. 'That's what I want for our baby.' Necessary

'My mum got pregnant with me when she was 16 and she had a tough time,' said Jeff, pointing out that he and Jade were both raised in one-parent families. 'Now I'm looking forward to bringing someone new into the world myself. I want to be totally involved and experience everything. I'll be there all the time and will be very proud. I doubt Jade will be the best nappy-changer in the world but I'll be happy to muck in.'

It all sounded fantastic and once the shock had passed the couple decided the future looked pretty bright. Jade called Jeff her 'knight in shining armour' and her 'soulmate' and they talked late into the night about how they would look after and care for their child, and how lucky they were to be together. They also worked out that, if they shared the burden and had enough support from their families and friends, they would be able to take it in turns to keep on working and earning once the baby had arrived. Suddenly things didn't look so bad and the pair started to get excited about the challenges that were to come.

But, unhappily, all these calm, optimistic and exciting thoughts were soon to disappear because pregnancy wasn't easy on Jade – or on Jeff. 'People often say that women blossom during pregnancy but I didn't feel that way. I was absolutely terrible,' admitted Jade afterwards, saying her hormones drove her wild and dramatically affected her behaviour. 'I was always having a go at Jeff. I never ever thought of his feelings. I'd say things I didn't mean. Really nasty things that hurt him. We'd argue almost every day because having a baby is a strain. Me being who I am is a strain. I always said you need to be a lunatic to live with me, and pregnancy made everything even worse.'

News of Jade's pregnancy had dominated the papers and celebrity magazines for weeks when it had first been revealed. Now those same papers and magazines were ready to report on the rows that were breaking out between the couple with ever increasing regularity. Luckily, Jeff was still committed to being with Jade – mood swings or no mood swings. And Jade soon realised how lucky she was to be with him.

'Jeff still had the patience to care about my feelings and put his feelings aside,' said Jade years later, when she analysed the way she had behaved as a pregnant woman. Jeff was also prepared to add some unorthodox items to the couple's weekly shopping list – because Jade's food cravings in pregnancy were typically off the wall. Haribo sweets and ham were top of her list for a while. Before that, pickled-onion-flavour Monster Munch dipped in hummus had been all she felt like eating.

Meanwhile, Jade's mum was thrilled that she was going to become a grandmother – and was over the moon that her daughter was set to raise a child in a stable two-parent, double-income home. Jackiey was ready to pitch in with any babysitting duties so that Jade could carry on working, and she was busy building a strong friendship with Jeff's side of the family to ensure her daughter's support network extended as far as possible.

But, as if Jade and Jeff didn't have enough on their plates, they had also decided to move house – to a new £300,000 home in the far from glamorous Essex town of Harlow. For someone who had spoken about moving to London's celebrity enclave Primrose Hill after hitting the financial jackpot after *Big Brother*, the move to Harlow came as something of a surprise. At first glance the modern London-overspill town doesn't have much going for it. It has been called one of Britain's ugliest and least charming towns – the kind of place anyone with money tries to leave rather than the other way round. But a closer examination shows the area has played host to rather more big names than most people imagine. Former England and Spurs manager Glenn Hoddle was born there, and the town and its many pretty neighbouring villages are popular with minor Spurs stars, as well as past and present *EastEnders* actors including Michael French and Des Coleman. Meanwhile, there is some real star power just up the road. The Beckhams live a few miles north in Sawbridgeworth and, surprisingly enough, Victoria was frequently spotted taking Brooklyn and Romeo for a quick meal at Harlow's town-centre Pizza Hut. While their parents may prefer places like The Ivy in London's West End, this was the boys' favourite restaurant, friends say. Slightly to the east of Harlow itself is another, more infamous, celebrity home – the villa-style property of troubled comedian Michael Barrymore, who hosted the tragic late-night party that ended when local butcher Stuart Lubbock drowned in the swimming pool.

Jade was a big fan of the area from day one. 'I really like it here,' she told BBC Essex reporter Simon Baldock shortly after moving in. 'I wake up every morning to the smell of fresh air and there are really nice people here. I do feel at home.'

Her new neighbours were keen to repay the compliment. 'Jade is not exactly typical of the normal residents here, to say the least. But she is being made to feel very welcome and we are happy to have her,' said one posh stockbroker neighbour.

In time, Jade was to find out that she had probably done her future a lot of favours by buying exactly the right sort of property – at exactly the right time. Financial experts say investing in bricks and mortar almost always makes sense. 'When we look at the source of wealth of so many of Britain's richest people, one word pops up more often than any other: property,' said journalist Toby Walne, who has worked on the annual Rich Reports published by the *Mail on Sunday*. 'High prices mean the average first-time buyer is now 34. Jade has got an enormous head start by buying at 22.'

Unfortunately, the media wasn't prepared to leave Jade and Jeff alone to prepare for their new lives in peace. Papers had lapped up stories about the couple's arguments, and in April 2003 the *Daily Star* went further and claimed that Jade was going to spend £3,000 to have her baby at the private Portland Hospital in London, where Victoria Beckham gave birth. An unnamed 'close family friend' told the *Star* that Jade was snubbing the NHS and worrying her family.

'What's wrong with using the NHS like the rest of us?' the so-called friend asked. 'This isn't the Jade I know – she's changed. I never would have thought she would do something like this. Jade's always used the NHS before, so I don't see why she has to pay £3,000 just to have her baby in a private hospital. It's absolutely crazy – and I'm not the only one who feels this is wrong. Several others are very surprised at the way she is spending her money. We're not saying she is stingy because she has been really generous – but it's the way she is wasting her money.'

As it turned out, Jade didn't go to the Portland Hospital after all. She gave birth in her local NHS hospital in Harlow. And this wasn't the only false rumour put about by the papers that spring. The same 'close family friend' who said Jade was 'too posh to push on the NHS' had also said her baby would be called Archie, if it was a boy. Wrong again. What even the doctors got wrong was Jade's due date. She actually went into labour exactly four weeks earlier than scheduled – the opposite of many first-time mums who often give birth late.

Jade was rushed to hospital with Jeff and mum Jackiey, and she stayed in labour for nine hours, trying to use as few drugs as possible to ensure the birth was as natural as it could be. And, like all births, the event itself was life-changing for all concerned. 'When I saw his head I couldn't stop myself from crying, it was the most overwhelming, emotional thing,' Jeff told *OK!* magazine when they asked him about the birth.

The couple's baby weighed just 5 lb and 7 oz, was to be called Bobby Jack, and neither Jade nor Jeff wanted him out of their arms. But nature wasn't going to let them play happy families just yet. Like many premature babies, Bobby was going to trigger a few health scares in his first few hours. He was weak, had jaundice and needed to rest on a heated mattress under a sunlamp in the neonatal intensive care unit while he tried to gather his strength and recover.

Doctors say mums can have problems bonding with premature babies – not least because early, underweight babies aren't always the most attractive of creatures. They tend to be more wrinkled than full-term babies, with big heads that look out of proportion with the rest of their tiny bodies. When you do get to hold premature babies they can feel bony and they often appear to be having difficulty breathing, even when everything is actually all right. Midwives say the isolation you feel when a newborn baby has to go into an incubator can also trigger extra worries for both parents. So it was a tough few days while Jade and Jeff watched and waited to find out when Bobby would be well enough to go home.

Nurses and fellow patients at the Essex hospital said the couple were clearly worried about their new son's health – but desperately excited about the future. 'They doted on him from the start and couldn't take their eyes off him when they were with the lad,' said one. 'They might have looked worried when they talked to the medical staff sometimes, but as soon as they looked at their baby they began smiling.'

And, despite being exhausted, Jade had certainly not lost her sense of humour. 'I hope he gets his dad's brains and not mine,' she joked with one fellow mum. Fortunately, once the couple were given the all-clear to take little Bobby home he began to thrive. And back in their new house in Essex the trio settled down to the new routines of family life – which they were determined to handle on their own.

'We don't want a nanny because we want to bring Bobby up ourselves, not leave him with someone else all the time,' said Jade. 'We're very lucky that with our work we will often be able to take him with us. And if there is a time I can't take him then he will be able to stay with Jeff and vice versa.' Both parents found they loved having a baby around as a focus for their energies and attentions. But they both admitted that interrupted nights and heavy new responsibilities were adding to the teething troubles of their still new relationship. Part of the problem was that the couple hadn't just had a baby and moved house – two of the most stressful events in our lives, according to experts. They had also started a risky new business.

Earlier that year, unknown to the press and television reporters who seemed to spend their lives following Jade's every move, the mum-to-be had enrolled in the Brentwood Academy of Health and Beauty, and was training to be a qualified beautician. Working in the beauty business had been an ambition of hers since her early childhood and today it was what she called her 'top-secret fall-back plan' to protect her in case her media career stalled. Apparently one of the other ladies on the professional course told Jade she looked 'just like that girl from *Big Brother*' but Jade tried to keep the truth under wraps so she could get her qualifications in private. Regrettably, someone tipped off the press and a freelance photographer snapped her walking into class one day in her regulation white coat.

'So, are you turning your back on fame?' she was asked when the story broke. For once, Jade's answer was guarded. 'I'd like to think that there will be more TV and other spin-offs,' she said carefully. 'But I'm always waiting for the bubble to pop. So I'm training as a beauty therapist in case it does all dry up. I've always wanted my own business and now I can afford to do it. It's a goal. I'm going to set up a beauty salon with an old friend.'

After throwing herself into the course work while pregnant, Jade managed to pass the exams in some style. And her new beauty qualifications led almost directly to what for a while became the country's most famous tanning salon – the Sunbed Shop in South Woodford, Essex. This was the big business new parents Jade and Jeff set up towards the end of 2003, and photographs of Jade putting out 'opening soon' signs in the early morning were splashed across the papers to ensure a busy first few weeks of trading.

In a high-rent location, with big fixed costs to cover, it was a huge financial gamble for the couple. But Jeff shared his professional and personal partner's sanguine attitude to fame and the future, so he was convinced it was a risk worth taking. 'You can never tell in this business,' he said when asked about his own television and media career. 'I really love presenting, but the problem with this kind of work is that one minute you can have loads of it, then you might have none and people have forgotten about you. We've been fortunate until now and we still have lots coming up, but you just never know what will happen in the future. So it is good to have something to fall back on and a sun-tanning shop seemed a good bet.'

Fortunately, neither Jeff nor Jade was afraid of hard work and both were running the business for real, not just putting on some show for the cameras outside. 'Me and Jade take turns working in the shop, answering the phones and serving customers, so it's a proper family business,' said Jeff. 'Jade's brilliant. She doesn't mind working hard and, between us, we have everything covered. It is hard work but that's how you get the rewards. I didn't intend to make our working lives more hectic, but I am convinced it will be a good thing. I really hope it takes off.'

Unfortunately, before it did there were a lot of hours to put in. And this added to the pressure on its two managers. So after a few quiet months getting used to having Bobby around, tension started mounting and the couple's rows and shouting matches became the stuff of tabloid legend once more. They both fought in public, as well as in private, and for a while it looked as if they would be apart before Bobby celebrated his first Christmas at six months old.

Jade, however, was convinced that their relationship could last the course – and that their rows were a healthy part of growing up. 'Yes, we have arguments, but that's normal,' she said when asked about yet another public bust-up. 'This is real life and we're not going to pretend. The only difference between us and other people is that there are photographers hanging around the house to take pictures of Jeff when he storms out.'

You might think that Jade and Jeff would have been free from the paparazzi when they were in Essex, but that was far from true. With so many celebrity magazines on offer, there is a voracious demand for pictures. Years ago the market was such that photographers would only take outstanding posed snaps of famous people looking fantastic and would ignore them at all other times. Nowadays this is not the case. Photographers know they may be more likely to sell a picture of a big name looking dreadful and putting out the rubbish than they would of the same star dressed up to the nines at an opening night or a film première. Our recent love of 'unguarded moment' shots of celebrities eating, drinking, looking rough or having arguments means it really is worthwhile for photographers to spend all day hanging round celebrities' homes on the off chance that they will get an unusual angle. And with 'Beckingham Palace' just up the road, many felt it was always useful stopping off outside the Goody house as part of their working day.

Jade, for one, tries to put things in perspective and not let the constant attention from photographers bother her. 'I think it goes with the job really. If you are doing something that has made you famous then you should just accept that there will be photographers waiting outside your home when you walk out in the morning. It happens a lot and now I just walk outside and say, "Hello, what are you doing here now?" Then I just go off and do what I have to do.'

The only time Jade did find the pictures a problem was when she and Jeff were fighting – because she thought it ended up giving a bad impression of what was, most of the time, a pretty strong relationship at that point. She herself was gradually managing to take these rows in her stride, and no longer saw them as a real threat to the couple's future. 'You need to let off steam sometimes. I'm an argumentative person but Jeff isn't. He's like my anger-management teacher,' she said, trying to analyse their situation and discover what made their relationship work.

Luckily, Jeff seemed happy with the role of peacemaker. 'Our personalities are quite opposite but it works well. We're actually really good for each other,' he said. 'She brings me out of myself and I can shut her up when she starts on one. We argue non-stop but we love each other to pieces. She's really changed my life.'

For her part, Jade was keenly aware of how lucky she was – even if life Goody-style was sometimes a little unusual. 'I always wanted the big house, the big career, the marriage and then the baby. I've just done it all the wrong way round,' she admitted. And for a while it looked as if it could be happy ever after for the famously volatile couple. A magazine interviewer asked Jade what her perfect romantic evening would be. She replied, 'Simple stuff, really. I'd like Jeff cooking a nice meal for me, with lots of candles and a babysitter for Bobby.'

Sadly, it seemed that when Jade and Jeff were alone together a new row was never far from the surface. Jade's life was about to get even tougher. And the tabloids and the gossip magazines were going to milk it for all it was worth.

chapter 10

Beat That, Madonna

'Hello, everyone, I'm Jade.'

Sunday Mirror reporter Deirdre O'Brien said it is just as well that the stylish, svelte person that strolled into the photographic studio early that morning in January 2004 had identified herself so clearly. 'Although I had spent many hours observing Jade Goody on the small screen, I wasn't entirely sure it was really her,' said Deirdre. 'The shrill South London accent is the same, but the rest of her has undergone a dramatic transformation – into a toned yet curvy figure clad in trendy clothes with glossy, dark hair that tumbles around her shoulders.'

And Deirdre said this even before the professional hair stylists, dressers, make-up artists and photography assistants had done their magic for the *M* Celebs fashion shoot she was overseeing.

As the crew composed themselves and prepared to start work, Jade was busy getting ready herself. Photographic studios had long since started to feel like her second home – and, if baby Bobby had been old enough to speak, he would probably have said the same. That day Bobby was there with his mum as usual. Jade was refusing to employ a nanny or even an au pair, as she felt that children are best looked after by family members, so Bobby smiled a big gummy grin at the professionals as he crawled happily around their workspace for the duration of the shoot.

Jade's agents had arranged to have a near constant series of new photos taken of their client, an essential activity for someone who had become one of the most unlikely, but successful, magazine-cover stars in Britain. At first Jade found it hard to relax in front of the cameras. She was also intimidated by the sheer professionalism of the process. The typical magazine photo shoot is now an increasingly complicated affair. Small studios tend to be crammed with as many as a dozen different people, all demanding a share of the action and a piece of their model's attention. Mobile phones ring, meetings are called, arguments break out and voices can be raised. And as a model you have to stay calm and focused in the eye of the storm.

'People say it is easy to stand around all day having your photo taken, but you only have to try it to realise that the pressure can soon take its toll,' says model Tamsin Baker, who has appeared on the cover of everything from *Bella* to *That's Life* magazine. 'In most shoots you are acting a role and have to turn on the same intensity for every shot. People think we just have to show up, wait till the photographer has used a roll of film and then head to the bank with our cheques. In reality models have to wait through endless delays while the vast number of people around us decide what they want to get out of the shoot. And most of the time we have to pretend we agree with them even if we know they'll probably change their minds and start all over again in the next half-hour.'

From the moment Jade left the *Big Brother* set she says she fell in love with the manic atmosphere found in many photography studios. More importantly, the studio staff fell in love with her.

'It sounds like a cliché, but photographers and art directors do like a blank canvas to work on,' says freelance stylist Samantha Tate. 'You don't want to just repeat the same shots that the guy who took pictures the previous week produced and that's why everyone's favourite models are the ones who scrub up well and can look different every day.'

Jade certainly fell into that category. And, as luck would have it, almost anything she did in her first professional photo shoots was going to wow the public – because everyone had got so used to seeing her looking pretty dreadful without make-up in the *Big Brother* house.

Celebrity make-up artist Sally Cairns, who has worked with pop stars Liberty X and Atomic Kitten as well as a host of other cover stars, took a close interest in Jade's potential as a cover star in her first few months of fame. She said Jade had several things in her favour but needed to work hard to keep her flawless new image intact. 'Luckily Jade is a girlie, girlie and enjoys make-up and beauty. She's now been treating herself to manicures and pedicures so she's glossy and groomed. Her only challenge is not to go mad on the partying as it will affect her skin as she is prone to spots. Too many late nights and hangover-cure fry-ups won't do her any favours,' she said.

Jade, typically, was ready to listen. Once more she saw her first few photo shoots as a giant learning experience. She would do what she was told, pay attention to what was going on, and find out what could turn an ordinary woman into a hot property. But she was also ready to have some fun.

To this day she says one of her favourite photo shoots was the one for the *News of the World*, when she was turned into Marilyn Monroe for an afternoon. The idea was to turn Jade from a voluptuous, blonde former housemate into a voluptuous, blonde love goddess. The sexy transformation worked perfectly – and Jade couldn't have been happier. Dressing up had always been a favourite pastime. And now she was getting help from the professionals and being paid for the experience. It was hard to see how life could get much better – especially when her favourite stars from the past were being involved. 'Marilyn is such an icon. I loved being her and I bet she would have had a wicked time in the *Big Brother* house,' she said.

Getting help with knowing what to wear was another huge bonus of fame. Fashion experts were always on hand with advice as Jade went from one media appearance to another. *Daily Star* fashion editor Sam Howard-Phillips warned her against bright, bold colours as they can emphasise unflattering lumps and bumps. He pointed out that Jade's surprisingly long legs are one of her hidden assets and suggested she show them off with long, straight dresses that finished at the knee. When she wanted to look more business-like and polished he recommended trouser suits where the jackets finish at the hips rather than the waist, saying that these make women of Jade's build look leaner and taller than they really are.

But, for all the professional advice from top stylists, Jade admits that she will probably never have the unerring fashion and style sense of some of her heroines such as the actress Angelina Jolie. A reporter once asked Jade if she thought she had made many fashion blunders since leaving the *Big Brother* house. She held up her hand and admitted it with a laugh. 'There was one outfit that was in the "bling" columns but I reckon it was more "ming",' she said. 'It was an '80s-style dress from Topshop with squares on it. I had my hair in a funky style with huge earrings and pink shoes. What was I thinking?'

And as the years go by she is also learning to accept her physical shortcomings. When talking about her New Year's resolutions she said, 'One day I was trying to work out why so many people laugh at me. Then I saw myself on television and I was dressed in the kind of clothes that the stars in Liberty X would wear, and I'm at least two sizes too big for them. So my New Year's resolution is to wear clothes that actually fit me.'

Ask her where she shops and you soon realise that the Bermondsey girl hasn't entirely forgotten her roots, though. She says she loves the big designers such as Gucci, Dolce & Gabbana, Karen Millen and Armani – and she particularly loves the fact that she can finally afford to buy their clothes. But Jade enjoys spending a few hours going through the racks of Topshop, French Connection and H&M just as much.

Jade also loves being styled for a fashion layout. She says she gets a real thrill out of looking at racks of clothes and accessories that are laid out for her by magazine fashion editors. If you do enough shoots, you're likely to be given the chance to take some of the merchandise home with you as an extra thank-you present as well. And from the moment she left the *Big Brother* house Jade started to do more shoots than almost anyone had expected.

Julian Stockton from Outside, the management company that temporarily looks after contestants post-*Big Brother*, said the media interest in Jade was absolutely unprecedented. 'It is completely up to the contestants to decide if they want to appear in the press at all after the show,' he said. 'We just put the offers in front of them and tell them the pros and cons of each. The final decisions are always left up to the contestants. Some of the housemates don't want to and that is 100 per cent fine. For those who are willing, the norm is that they might do one story and photo shoot for a newspaper and one for a magazine.'

In the early days of her fame, Jade, of course, ended up doing one set of stories and photo shoots for a newspaper and one set for a magazine every few days. And demand for her image has not abated as the years have gone by. Critics said she wouldn't even last until the end of the fabled 15 minutes of fame. But Jade has proved them all wrong.

Against all the odds Jade has turned into – and remains – one of Britain's most prolific magazine-cover girls. Her face has been on everything from *Now* and *Closer* to *OK!*, *Heat* and all of the glossy supplements that come with the weekend papers. Some weeks Jade can be seen smiling out

Top: Jade proves that carrying a baby around doesn't stop her from looking glamorous – and thin.

Above: Back from Mothercare in a Porsche – just what you would expect for Britain's first reality television millionairess.

Love the hat – Jade goes up
in the world at Royal Ascot.

witch outfit
£8

Top: Shopping for a witch's costume for an episode of *The Paul O'Grady Show*.

Above left: Happy as ever, Jade ropes in a passer-by to help with her gardening.

Above right: Proud gran Jackiey with Bobby Jack at Jade's Essex home.

Top: Keeping close friend Paul O'Grady captivated on his ITV chat show.

Above: Laughing along with Michelle Collins – Jade has now been a guest on almost every major television chat show.

mming it up with *Back to Reality* co-star Catalina.

Top: Singing and getting a soaking on the *Ministry of Mayhem* kid's show.

Above left: Jade soaks up the sun at the tenth V Festival in Essex.

Above right: Jade's sleek bob turns heads as she arrives at the 2006 Brit Awards.

Top: A very public kiss for Ryan Amoo. Things got too serious too quickly for
Jade and they split after only six months.

Above: Jade with her first-born son Bobby Jack on the *Paul O'Grady Show*.

A slimline Jade heads
out to face the future.

from as many as three major magazines at a time in newsagents. And that's no accident. Jade goes on the covers for one simple reason: her face sells.

'The magazine world is a cut-throat business and what you put on the cover is vitally important,' says media analyst Anthony Barnes, who is brought in to help ailing publications enjoy a new lease of life. 'The wrong look or the wrong celebrity on a women's weekly magazine can dramatically hit sales if it loses the vital impulse buyers one week. This is a very professional industry and the magazines know what works and what doesn't. If a star doesn't shift magazines, they won't be used again. But if someone is asked back then you know for sure that they've got the X-factor. They're single-handedly persuading people to buy a magazine, which is no mean feat when there is so much choice out there.'

As far as Jade is concerned, she can persuade people to buy magazines in their tens of thousands. *Heat* magazine is the perfect example. It has been a massive sales success since its troubled launch in 1999, and it has acquired a tough reputation as one of the most hard-nosed, professional and demanding of the celebrity titles. Editor Mark Frith is credited with having an almost unerring instinct for what celebrity fans want to see and read about. And he says that most of the time this is Jade Goody, rather than the likes of Madonna, Brad Pitt or even the home-grown Victoria Beckham.

'Madonna is the one you might want to be, but Jade is the one you identify with,' said Frith, explaining why he wants Jade's face on so many of his magazine covers. 'The people who buy celebrity magazines would quite simply rather read about Jade than about a global megastar such as Tom Cruise, for example. I could spend the next year of my life trying to get an interview with Cruise, but all the guy would tell me is how great it was to work with his latest director. Jade, on the other hand, would tell me everything, about her body image, her relationship, her career, her hopes and ambitions. The result? Readers identify with Jade, not Tom Cruise.'

So it is Jade who goes on the magazine's front cover – again and again. Jade is still *Heat* magazine's best-selling cover star ever, in one week having helped shift a staggering 655,000 copies of a magazine that can sell far less than 540,000 copies when a lesser star gets top billing, for instance. And, while you might think that a more established name like Madonna, Jennifer Lopez, Cameron Diaz, Geri Haliwell or Victoria Beckham would have rung up the most cover photographs in the past three years, that accolade goes to Bermondsey girl Jade – who wins the fame race by a mile. Her picture or her name featured on an amazing 14 *Heat* magazine covers in 2004 alone – that's an average of more than one top-selling front cover every month.

Other magazines have found similar magic in Jade's image. Best-selling celebrity magazine *OK!* has also found that Ms Goody can attract more buyers than almost anyone else. Several of the many dozens of issues where Jade has been on the cover are now sold out, unavailable even through the company's efficient and normally well-stocked back-issues department.

It is little wonder, then, that Jade would be top of the magazine's list of potential cover stars when *OK!* was approaching its 10th anniversary in December 2003 and was planning a 'Special Collectors' Edition'. Celebrity couples Catherine Zeta Jones and Michael Douglas and Victoria and David Beckham were also on the shortlist, alongside British model Jordan. But in the end *OK!* decided that these five huge stars would have to make do with modest pictures along the bottom of the landmark front cover. Pride of place in the main picture were three other people – Jade, Jeff and new baby Bobby. 'Jade at home: World Exclusive' screamed the front cover – giving a taster of the 11 pages and 17 pictures that dominated the magazine in that most high profile of weeks.

Jade knew full well that getting ready for an 'at home' photo shoot like this can be hard work – but great fun. The challenge is to ensure that your house looks as good as you do, which means opening your doors to an army of interior-design experts and stylists as well as the usual hair and make-up staff. Some celebrities also manage to drive a hard bargain out of some furniture companies in the process – asking for a free or cut-price home makeover in return for mentioning a few brand names in the accompanying interviews.

Jade and Jeff, however, had a quite different and far less mercenary priority when they agreed to these sorts of photo shoots. They just wanted some fantastic new baby photos for Bobby's album. 'You really cannot beat a professionally taken and properly lit photograph,' says celebrity snapper John Armitage. 'Most new parents go to their local photographic studio for some shots and parents always treasure the official pictures taken of their children at school. Celebrities are no different – they just get the chance to have some more natural images taken in their homes as well. People sometimes say famous people must have no pride if they open themselves up to the media that much, when in fact the opposite can sometimes be true. New parents are often so proud of their children that they jump at the chance to show them off and the actual shoots, while chaotic, can be really touching affairs.'

Jade herself was sometimes at a loss to explain the public's fascination with her life, or the reason why she was asked to star in so many photo shoots and give so many interviews. 'I'm not famous, I'm not a celebrity, not a star. I'm just a face people will recognise,' she said in the early days of the media storm that swirled around her. And it turned out that it was this very innocent ordinariness that cemented her long-term appeal.

Psychologist Dr Glenn Wilson, reader in personality at the University of London's Institute of Psychiatry, said Jade is the epitome of the modern celebrity: someone who can at least start off by being famous just for being famous. 'She's also a vulnerable, child-like woman like Marilyn Monroe,' he said, little knowing at the time that Jade had just dressed up as exactly the same woman in her *News of the World* photo shoot and would years later be accused of having plastic surgery to resemble her heroine. 'Jade is effectively a representative of the downtrodden, of those who can't see any better future for themselves. They think, She's right down at my level so if she can be famous then so can I.'

But Dr Wilson also reckons he knows how Jade has been able to turn public opinion round and move from being hated to loved. 'She has an emotional intelligence that allows her to turn what could have been a destructive experience to her advantage. Emotional intelligence is a mixture of knowing how to deal with your own emotions and a usually female sensitivity to other people's feelings. Jade also has the capacity to be unguarded when describing her own feelings in areas where most might have inhibitions.'

That's something Dr Wilson says Jade has in common with the late Princess Diana – someone who knew more than most about the relentless demands and pressures of the modern media. Others agreed that Jade's character and her background made people feel closer to her than they did to other more polished stars.

'Jade is volatile with strong emotions very near the surface, meaning her antics are unpredictable and often entertaining. And she has no qualms about cheerfully mining her own life for every penny,' says *Daily Express* show-business writer Gill Swain, when trying to explain the media's unprecedented fascination with Jade. 'In an era when celebrities only give bland interviews and exert total control over their portrayal, the media seizes on characters like Jade, whose life story provides a benchmark against which readers can measure their own experiences.'

Amazingly enough, it wasn't just readers in Britain who wanted to use Jade as a benchmark against which to judge their own lives. The girl from Bermondsey wasn't exactly a global phenomenon. But she did still make headlines around the world. Perhaps to Britain's shame, it all began when the tabloids began their unprecedented hate campaign in bid to have her ousted from the *Big Brother* house. Papers in countries as far apart as Germany, Japan and America reported on the phenomenon, as an example of how cruel and out of control Britain's once-proud newspaper industry had become.

In Australia, where Pom-bashing is a national pastime, the story got even more coverage and Jade was held up as the classic victim of posh prejudice back in the old country. She was also seen as something else most Aussies love – an embattled underdog fighting for survival against the cruel and uncaring British establishment.

'We have our own *Big Brother* in Australia but the British version is always in the news here as well because we watch a lot of British television and have a lot of British expats in the country,' said Hilary Bloomfield, who has worked on the picture desk of many of the country's best-selling celebrity magazines. 'And Jade was always guaranteed more coverage than you might expect for someone who is neither famous nor Australian because her pictures looked so good on the page. Everyone used the first ones to show how awful she was and to illustrate all the "pig" stories. Then we were able to follow up with her new look. She's seen as the ugly duckling who has turned into a swan, and that's a very powerful and memorable storyline for readers to buy into.'

And what a swan Jade had turned out to be. Her photo shoots became increasingly glamorous as she gained confidence in herself and the team she was building around her. The world of celebrity hair, make-up and beauty artists is actually a relatively small one and Jade often seeks out her favourites – and is happy to see them paid big money in return for making her look sensational. A top make-up artist can bill for as much as £1,000 per photo session, according to magazine insiders, and the best hairstylists will want even more – plus expenses.

But, while Jade might look better than the average supermodel in her most recent fashion spreads and cover shots, there were always those who wanted to dredge up the past and remind everyone of how her journey had begun. 'Scientists have found that a pig's orgasm lasts for 30 minutes,' reported the *Sun* in July 2003 just after a stunning new set of photos had been released to the media. 'But *Big Brother*'s Jade Goody has refused to comment.'

Fortunately, Jade was now able to laugh at comments like this along with everyone else. And she was always ready to laugh at herself as well. After posing for pictures in chic evening dresses, she was asked what she would serve for a dream New Year's Eve party, for instance. Her reply was typical Jade. 'For starters I'd have smoked salmon and caviar, and for mains we'd have kebab and chips with chilli sauce. To finish we'd enjoy profiteroles. I can't spell them, but I do know how to make them.'

The newly confident Jade had also long since forgiven Graham Norton for the mauling he had given her while she was in the *Big Brother* house. 'I know he said horrible things about me but he was just doing his job,' she said realistically. It was the same with the newspaper editors who had begun the brutal anti-Jade campaigns. 'If I had an umbrella, I would bash you over the head with it. But, to be honest, I didn't take much notice of it all,' she said jokingly to former *Daily Mirror* editor Piers Morgan when he read Jade some of the most unpleasant things his paper had written about her during the programme. 'Why should all that bother me? You were only doing what you were paid for.'

Morgan himself admitted that when he first met her he had been enchanted by the woman his paper had attacked with such venom. 'Jade was refreshingly honest, a sweetie,' he said after filming her for his BBC One series *Tabloid Tales*. 'At that point she hadn't read any of the outrageous "Get this fat pig out of there" press coverage. So I showed her the clips and read her the journalistic poison. And she laughed and laughed. And pointed out that, since she has endured endless taunts about her dad spending most of her life in prison and her mum being a one-armed lesbian, why should the *Mirror*'s Kevin O'Sullivan calling her a Michelin-sized fishwife bother her? Jade has never complained and in the end I think that says more about her than it does about the tabloids.'

Jade had in fact found a uniquely clever way to deal with the fact that she had been called a pig for so long. 'I have decided Pig means Pretty Intelligent Girl,' she said, putting a brave face on things once more. This sort of well-grounded sense of humour and an ability to laugh at herself was going to be pretty important to Jade in the next few years, because her life was going to get busier, more stressful and more high profile than ever before.

chapter 11

I'm a Celebrity Get Me on Here!

Against all the odds Jade Goody has become an expert at walking the narrow tightrope of celebrity. She has notched up an impressive list of television credits in a very short time – and decent audience figures mean she is constantly being asked back for more.

But experts say that forging a thriving television career like this is nowhere near as easy as it looks. Like the best Bushtucker trials that Ant and Dec introduce in *I'm A Celebrity – Get Me Out of Here!*, there are some great rewards on offer if you win the fame game. But you are likely to fade away into obscurity if you fail.

The challenge had begun pretty much the day Jade left the *Big Brother* house in the summer of 2002. She had to decide if she should go crazy and cash in on her sudden fame – taking every penny offered her, however awful the project – or if she should try and pace herself, and build some foundations for a solid, long-term media career. And, of course, Jade's first problem was that she was walking into pretty uncharted territory and she was all on her own. She had no family members in the entertainment industry, no famous friends who could tell her how to deal with the press and weigh up one media offer against another. All she had were her own instincts and her steely determination to make the most of the opportunities *Big Brother* had given her.

Super-agent and show-business guru Max Clifford was the first to say that Jade would have to find help – and that it was essential that she learned how to sort the good guys from the bad. 'Jade needs an agent who knows what programmes are coming up and who has the clout and the contacts to get her in there while she is hot,' he said. 'But she needs to do select interviews and television appearances so it is not overkill. It must be carefully controlled. It's quality rather than quantity that counts.'

Clifford then cited the example of other former housemates who had tried to move into a television career but who became overexposed and lost credibility after snapping up every party and television invitation they received. Once you get a reputation for turning up at the classic 'opening of an envelope', you can be written off as a joke and not even considered for serious presenting jobs, according to television insiders. 'For every former housemate the difference between success and failure will be good management,' said Clifford.

Thankfully, Jade's first fun steps into the media spotlight were all pretty harmless. Most of them came courtesy of the *Sun* – which had only weeks earlier been calling Jade 'the most hated woman in Britain'. Having realised that the public didn't agree, the paper changed its tune and took her back to her native Bermondsey on top of 'the *Sun* Bus' for an emotional reunion with family, friends and fans. It then took her to Cambridge – in the heart of the East Anglia she had famously called East Angular and had thought was abroad during *Big Brother*. 'It's great getting a chance to come here among all these brainboxes and even nicer to get such a warm welcome,' she cried from a punt where she dressed up in a mortar board and gown. 'I really enjoy ponting – I mean punting.'

Other big-money offers were also mounting up. 'The phone hasn't stopped ringing,' said proud mum Jackiey, who had entered the Goody clan into a television company's competition to find a Simpsons-style family for a new show. 'Nasty people said Jade was thick but she'll have the last laugh.'

One private company was trying to buy the rights to host corporate gatherings at the old *Big Brother* house, for example. It wanted to pay Jade £1,500 an hour to show VIP guests around it. And it reckoned it would need her for four hours a day to get maximum mileage out of the opportunity. Nightclub owners across the country were equally desperate to get Jade through their doors. '*Big Brother*'s popularity was all down to Jade and fans will flock to see her,' said John Bunce, manager of the Ikon, Diva and Bonds nightclubs in Coventry which rushed to sign her up. 'But we may have to send her a map just to make sure she knows where Coventry is.' Other clubs, from the south coast of England to Northern Ireland, all demanded similar visits from Britain's best-known 21-year-old. Some were prepared to pay as much as £1,000 a time for her presence. And experts say that in just six months Jade is likely to have earned nearly £55,000 from a massive round of personal appearances. That was the equivalent of nearly four years' work in her former role as a dental nurse.

Meanwhile, other firms also tried to ride the wave of Jade's new-found fame for nothing. The publishing company Chambers sent her one of its dictionaries – the *Chambers Primary Dictionary*, to be exact. They had apparently underlined some key definitions such as 'Rio de Janeiro', 'East Anglia', 'asparagus' and 'scapegoat'. 'The books are aimed at the 7 to 11 age group,' a Chambers spokesperson said with gentle humour. On pretty much the same theme, British Airways allegedly got on the phone to offer Jade free flights around the world to help her brush up on her geography. An American company had even seen Jade's unlikely potential as a model. The girl who had been called a pig was suddenly taking on roles more usually given to the likes of Kate Moss or Claudia Schiffer. 'As worn by Jade Goody' appeared on the previously unknown US firm Smashing Grandpa's website to help sell the 'Orgasm' vest Jade had worn on *Big Brother* and which British women were apparently desperate to buy as the show drew to a close.

Other modelling jobs were slightly less savoury, however. 'I got offered £1 million to strip off by a newspaper when I came out of the *Big Brother* house, but it's just not me,' she admitted later. 'I wouldn't want to make my name by doing something sleazy.' Rumours that *Playboy* had made approaches about using Jade as a centrefold were also dismissed. And Jade said she would never take up Peter Stringfellow's alleged idea of employing her as a star lap dancer in his famous London club. 'I really don't want to be seen as an exhibitionist,' she said, a little late, perhaps, bearing in mind that her live strip in the *Big Brother* house had been watched by millions and had been voted the most popular moment in the history of the show.

Among the other more mainstream offers was talk of a £100,000 deal to promote Hardcore Cider and another payment of £100,000 to present a *Big Brother* series in Australia, where Jade had already become big news after her treatment by the British press had been roundly condemned.

This final offer was one of many that never ultimately amounted to anything. But it had been an important proposal because Jade had decided that, if her media career was to take root, she would need to do more than just give newspaper interviews and pose for magazine front covers. What she really needed was to get back on television and stay there.

Immediately after *Big Brother* had ended, she had sat down and giggled her way though interviews on the sofa for the likes of *This Morning* and a selection of other daytime television shows. And then, of course, came Graham Norton. The Irish chat-show host had effectively kicked off and fuelled the tabloid hate campaign against Jade by running through her latest antics or statements on a nightly basis in every show. On the positive front, he, almost more than anyone else, made sure everyone knew Jade's name. The downside, however, was that he had also made her a laughing stock and his earliest comments about her were extraordinarily tough. He had slowly turned into Jade's biggest fan and supporter, rather than her main tormentor. That's why he was outside the *Big Brother* house (with a film crew alongside him) to meet her when she was finally evicted. That's why he was so pleased that Johnny Depp had supported her in the special video message. And that's why he then had Jade on his show a record number of consecutive evenings in her first week outside the house.

This gave Jade just a little bit more vital experience of what to expect inside a television studio, and as well as answering his questions and chatting along with other guests she proved she was still game for a laugh. Under the eye of fellow guests such as Alison Moyet, Brenda Blethyn and Ursula Andress, Jade happily took part in a series of tasks Graham and his team had devised. The tasks all poked fun at her Jade-isms, reminded viewers of some of her most eye-catching moments in the house and looked like great fun to film. But behind the scenes, however, Graham said all was not going as smoothly as it seemed. 'Jade emerged early on as the biggest personality and much has been made by journalists about how I was horrible and then nice about her. But it is very straightforward. At the beginning of *Big Brother* I found her wildly annoying, but then, as the weeks went by, I became fond of her,' he wrote in his best-selling autobiography *So Me*.

Having Jade on his show turned out to be another matter, however. And it showed just how vulnerable Jade was and how easy it would have been for everything to have gone wrong in those first few days back in the real world. 'It was like an educational film on the perils of fame,' Graham wrote. 'On the Monday she was the sweet, gormless girl we had got to know on *Big Brother* but night after night she became more difficult and diva-ish. I don't blame her, I blame the PR people and agents she was surrounded by, who were pumping her full of shit.'

Jade, unfortunately, couldn't see it. 'Basically they are just here to look after me,' she said trustingly about her new advisers in the first few manic days after *Big Brother*. 'They're also my friends as well.' Mercifully, the public were going to get the chance to work out for themselves if Jade's advisers were friend or foe. Immediately after leaving the *Big Brother* house, production company Endemol decided there was enough mileage in the Jade Goody story to produce a whole show about her – *What Jade Did Next*. Interestingly enough, there was never even any talk of a show entitled 'What Kate Did Next' and no other *Big Brother* contestant has ever had a similar post-eviction show made about them.

Jade's show was designed to be fly-on-the-wall reality-TV heaven. The cameras followed her through 10 days of meetings and madness as newspaper and magazine groups put in ever-higher bids for her story, photographers and stylists battled to update her image and Jade and her mum tried to have a good laugh. We saw her meet publicists, agents and managers. We even saw her looking at some houses in London's refined and expensive Primrose Hill, where the likes of Jude Law and Gwyneth Paltrow live –

though in the end Jade made her excuses at the estate agents and left. The show aired in prime time on Channel 4 and attracted nearly three million viewers, a very respectable showing for a channel that was, at the time, happy with any weekday rating above the two-million mark.

The show also gave the world a few more choice Jade-isms to remember her by. 'What's a ferret? Is it a bird?' she asked at one point, when told that one of the small, hairy animals was to appear on Graham Norton's chat show with her. 'Saddam Hussein? Is he a boxer or something?' was another.

Other comedians were also keen to get in on the act and give Jade's fledgling career another useful boost. Avid Merrion, star of Channel 4's *Bo' Selecta!*, was one of them and he proceeded to provide further proof that Jade's sense of humour was second to none. Having tried to hijack Jade's eviction interview with Davina McCall the day *Big Brother* ended, Avid took on the role of a crazed stalker, chasing her down the street and jumping out on her in front of the cameras. And then he got even more personal. 'He went to my house and got knickers out of my drawers, and then he married a doll with my face on it. But I like him,' Jade said, happy to share screen time on the series with what were then far bigger celebrity names such as Mariella Frostrup, Penny Smith and, of course, Davina McCall.

While all this was going on, Jade had also accepted a short-term but highly paid role that would prove to be as nerve-wracking as it was lucrative. She was reported to be collecting an amazing £20,000 for just four weeks' work playing the wicked Queen Dumplena in *Snow White and the Seven Dwarfs* at the Woodville Halls Theatre in Gravesend, Kent – that worked out at just over £1,000 for every hour of stage time.

'She's very expensive but we've broken box-office records because of her,' said producer John Spillers as his staff prepared to make Jade 'the wickedest queen ever'. Rehearsals were gruelling for someone who had no professional stage experience, struggled with scripts and had just realised she was pregnant. But all the effort turned out to have been worthwhile.

Jade loved being on stage in front of a live audience and the sell-out audiences turned out to love having her there – though they could hardly be called complementary. 'Give it up, Jade, you're a minger,' they screamed every night of the run, prompted by several cleverly written references in the panto script. And Jade took it all in her stride – knowing she had called herself a minger so many times that she could hardly complain when others followed suit. 'Getting booed is fun,' she said, slightly unconvincingly, after passing the first-night test with flying colours and getting a standing ovation from one of the wildest crowds the theatre had ever seen.

As a local heroine and the star of the town's big Christmas production, Jade was also the natural choice for one extra role. She was invited to turn on Gravesend's Christmas lights – not quite the honour of doing the job in London's Oxford Street, but not bad for someone who had been completely unknown less than nine months earlier.

In the New Year, however, with her first dance video filmed, promoted and selling well in the shops, Jade, though several months pregnant, was looking for a new challenge. She had just admitted in a magazine interview that she had bought a flash new car for Jeff and her family to use while she got round to taking her driving test. And this sparked some interested calls to her management company.

Producers putting together a show for the Comic Relief charity had come up with a bizarre idea for a one-off reality-TV series. It was going to be called *Celebrity Driving School* and they wanted to take a selection of non-driving famous names, film them being taught to drive and see if they could pass their tests – all in the full glare of the cameras. They got the champagne out when they realised that someone as high profile as Jade would qualify to be part of the show, and they cracked it open the day she signed up to take part.

As far as Jade was concerned, the show couldn't have been better. She needed to learn to drive, she wanted to stay on television and she was thrilled to be able to help a charity such as Comic Relief. As it turned out, she was also going to make some good friends during the shoot. When filming began, Jade was joined by the likes of *Pop Idol* runner-up Gareth Gates, actress and television presenter Nadia Sawalha, *EastEnders* star Natalie Cassidy and Lily Savage creator Paul O'Grady – someone who would turn out to be a great supporter in the future. On day one she also met her confident would-be instructor Rickie Wellbourn-Davies. The pair would hit it off from the start, though he didn't have an easy time on his hands when Jade sat in the driving seat of his car.

'I've been teaching people to drive for 26 years and I've

seen just about everything. But she is one of the hardest pupils I have ever had. She drives just like her personality – she's lairy and a bit of a live wire,' he concluded. 'She tends to lose concentration, looks at something and then forgets where she's going. Sometimes she's good, sometimes she's diabolical.'

You can say that again, Rickie, though of course every badly taken corner, stalled start or unexpected stop made fantastic, nerve-wracking television. And the theory test was particularly difficult for the woman who famously thought 'East Angular' was abroad and that Cambridge was in London. Jade failed. Three times.

Ever the gentleman, Rickie was still ready to make excuses for his star pupil, however. 'A lot of people say she's a thicko, but she's not,' he said, though he did admit that the phrase 'academically challenged' could have been created specially for her.

But Rickie also said that Jade had to overcome some unique hurdles when she was in the car. 'When you're driving along and someone shouts, "Oi, Jade", it's a little bit distracting for her,' he said. And terrifying for him and any nearby pedestrians, you would think – including BBC cameraman Jeremy Bishop and his director, who had to drop everything and leap into the bushes when Jade hit the accelerator instead of the brake on her three-point turn and mounted the kerb in her Ford Fiesta. 'I was on the pavement so I thought I was safe,' said Jeremy. 'I soon learned to give Jade a wider berth.'

'She made a pig's ear of the test,' Rickie admitted after Jade had failed. 'But I don't think she was really ready to

enter. She had 27 lessons. The average for passing is 40.'
And when the television cameras had gone, Rickie vowed
to be around to help Jade get her driving licence in private
if she ever has time for more lessons. 'I'd like to get her
through her test,' he says. 'And the way *Celebrity Driving
School* worked out hasn't put me off teaching her again. It's
actually given me more incentive because I like her.'

While Jade was spectacularly failing her three-point
turns, she was still winning fans in the head offices of some
of Britain's biggest and richest television production
companies. One firm in particular, RDF Media, was
absolutely certain that Jade was right for them. Among
other things, RDF produces the fantastically successful
Wife Swap show, where wives from two different families
move into each other's homes and lives for two weeks. In
the first week they have to follow the normal routine of the
home's real wife. In the second they can change things
however they see fit. It has made for riveting television as
we all get an inside view of how others run their personal
and domestic lives.

But in 2003 RDF Media had another idea – *Celebrity
Wife Swap*. And they wanted the pregnant Jade and her
partner Jeff Brazier to be one half of the swapping couples.
The others were to be equally controversial: upper-crust
Major Charles Ingram and his super-posh wife Diana, the
coughing couple who had been in court for attempting to
cheat on *Who Wants To Be A Millionaire?*.

'Both these couples are in the public eye and in both
cases people are interested in knowing a lot more about
them,' said RDF director of programmes Stephen Lambert.

'But we would have cast them even if they weren't famous. They would still be good people for *Wife Swap* because they come from completely different social backgrounds and see the world in very different ways. Swapping a young couple from London with a middle-aged couple with kids from Wiltshire would be a very good *Wife Swap* even if they weren't famous.'

The high profile of the leading players ensured that the show had even more spice than normal, however – with a high media profile to match. 'The minger meets the cheat,' proclaimed the *Guardian* when news of the show broke. And the omens, from the start, did not look good. 'When I agreed to do *Celebrity Wife Swap* I had never heard of my new "wife" Jade Goody,' said 40-year-old Charles. 'Nor had I seen *Big Brother*, the programme that had made her a star in 2002. Just a week before Jade was due to move in with me and my three daughters, I saw a programme about her on television and I was horrified. I couldn't believe what I had let myself in for. She seemed rude and obnoxious. I was terribly worried about the impact she would have on the children.'

Jade, then seven months pregnant, moved into the Ingrams' four-bedroom home in leafy Wiltshire – a world away from the gritty council estate in South London where she had been brought up. 'We had virtually nothing in common and Jade was a fish out of water in the countryside,' said Charles. 'I'm not sure she ever really grasped where Wiltshire is and all that stuff about her thinking "East Angular" is abroad isn't a joke. For the first three days we did everything by Di's rules and it was quite difficult for Jade. She's never known a real family environment, certainly not one this organised. She also couldn't understand why I was clock-watching. Jade didn't grasp that you just can't leave the girls at school for an extra 20 minutes, for example.'

Viewers weren't left in any doubt that Jade was the real victim of the situation, however. Charles Ingram was both a major and a man of the old school. Until he had been discharged from the army in disgrace after the attempted fraud on *Who Wants To Be A Millionaire?*, he had rarely been at home in the day and certainly never contributed to the cooking or the housework. His wife Diana, replaced by Jade, was left looking after three children and doing the cooking, cleaning, the school run, the washing and the ironing. The cooking in particular wasn't easy. Just after Jade arrived, Charles told her his family was coming round for Sunday lunch and she had to prepare a meal for nine, for example. Jade pulled it off, even though she had never lived in a house with more than three people in it before and was happy to admit that her domestic skills left a great deal to be desired.

Halfway through the *Celebrity Wife Swap* experience, however, Jade got the chance to call the shots and stamp her identity over the Ingram household. And again Charles wasn't happy. 'She announced that I was going to do everything around the house and she'd lie in bed until 10.30. I got really cheesed off and on day five I told her I thought things were out of order. And she just flew into a huge motormouth torrent. It was incredible. I was like a timid mouse standing in front of an alley cat. Her voice is amazing. It carries for miles and I kept thinking it would wake the kids.'

So, bad feelings all round? Surprisingly not. For all the initial worries and occasional flare-ups, both Jade and Charles managed to relax slightly in each other's company as the experiment continued. And Charles ended up doing what the whole nation had done a year earlier during *Big Brother* – he realised that against all the odds he had warmed to Jade. 'After our big row we started to get on like a house on fire and in the end I was really shocked by how nice Jade is,' he said. 'Though that's not to say that we weren't counting the days till the end of our two-week marriage. The children, fortunately, were a real ice-breaker at the start. They loved Jade and she was really good with them.'

Surprisingly, Jade managed to fit in pretty well amid the Ingrams' suburban, middle-class friends. 'The children were very excited about the prospect of her taking them to school,' said Charles. 'She talked to lots of mums and kids there, and they all seemed to respond very well to her. And while Jade is not well educated, she has bucket-loads of common sense. There's a lot I really admire about her. There aren't many other people who really know what it's like to go through media ridicule, but Jade understands. The tabloids branded her a pig and other ghastly things, and she's been able to laugh it off. She has been through the mangle in her life but she has come through it.'

Extraordinarily enough, Charles said there was a lot he could learn from his young housemate. 'She taught me how to deal with the press and how to relax. Everything that happens to her is water off a duck's back and there are a few lessons I can learn from that. She advised me a lot about becoming a millionaire and said I should treat the whole thing as a big joke, just like she has.'

Jade, who was well on her way to charming rather than cheating herself into a millionaire at this point, said Charles was also far nicer than she had expected. At one point she had even tried to give him a confidence boost by changing his image. 'You're 39 but you look like you're 49,' she said when she took him on a shopping trip. And she admitted that she too had learned a lot from the whole experience. 'At first I thought he would be a right plonker but Charles is nothing like I'd imagined him to be. I've certainly learned to stop judging people before I meet them,' was her conclusion when the odd couple finally parted with a surprisingly genuine hug.

Nearly six million viewers – a quarter of the total television audience that evening and the third highest total of the year for Channel 4 – were watching as the foursome went through the usual debriefing on their experiences and explained how, if at all, they would change their own behaviour afterwards.

Jade's own private reunion with Jeff, however, was a slightly tenser affair. All of Jade's old insecurities had resurfaced during the filming of the show. At 39, Diana Ingram may have been 15 years older than Jeff, but Jade was still terrified that he might be swept away by her or do something he shouldn't. 'I wasn't remotely worried about what Di and young Jeff might be getting up to,' said Charles after the show had been filmed and everyone was back in their rightful homes. 'But for Jade it was different.

She was clearly insecure that another woman was having a nice time with her boyfriend. I also think she was surprised how much she missed Jeff. She was caught using her mobile phone to him quite a few times, which was strictly against the rules, and she did spend a lot of time mooning about in the bedroom and being morose because she was worrying about him.'

Jeff, as viewers saw, wasn't going to have a fling with his temporary housemate – in fact, he went on so much about how 'old' she was that she had to ask him to change the subject. But he did have some fun – taking her to buy some new clothes and to some bars and nightclubs where, ever the gentleman, he said the 39-year-old could 'easily pass for someone in her thirties'. Interestingly, Jeff also seemed ready for some motherly advice. The pair sat and talked about life into the small hours some nights, finding far more common ground than they might have expected. Afterwards, Jeff said, 'The producers had put the two most temperamental people together, in Jade and Charles, so you knew there was going to be an explosive situation. But, as Diana and I are more laid-back, we quite enjoyed finding out about each other's lives. It was more difficult for Jade, but it was a good experience.'

When the show was over, Jade and Jeff could at least pay another healthy lump sum into their bank accounts. No one is saying exactly how much they were paid for the *Wife Swap* job, which lasted less than two weeks. But the far less famous newspaper journalist and author Toby Young and his wife Caroline said they had been offered the Charles and Diana Ingram role for a healthy fee of £30,000. In the end, Toby decided no amount of money could persuade him to leave his wife and spend even two weeks living under the same roof as Jade.

Back in her new home in Essex after the show, Jade wasn't letting motherhood get in the way of her career. She and Jeff were still working hard building up their sunbed business and were considering buying even more equipment and adding teeth-whitening to their growing list of services. New baby Bobby had grinned his way through several exclusive photo sessions – loving the attention he got from everyone on the shoots. And Jade was worried about her weight.

All the good work of the previous year had disappeared when she was pregnant and even after she had given birth she found she was back weighing pretty much the same as she had in the bad old days in the *Big Brother* house. She was also convinced that, if she didn't try to get back in shape fast, it would never happen. So she got ready to start dancing again and asked her managers if it was worth getting the cameras back round to record her. They jumped at the chance. Everyone had always wanted to make a follow-up to Jade's original exercise tape, and her dramatic weight gain with Bobby gave them the excuse to put the plan into action. If Jade really did get back in shape, then almost every other new mum in the country would want to know how she had done it. Another best-seller would be on the cards.

Jade's original choreographer, *Fame Academy*'s Kevin Adams, was busy on other projects, so the equally starry Paulette Minott was brought in instead – fresh from her work with Victoria Beckham and other chart stars Blue, Gabrielle, Mis-teeq and Sugababes. Paulette wanted a racier, pacier, more urban feel to the choreography and Jade had to get to grips with the new styles in less than six weeks. Rehearsals were long and tough but Jade loved the music, enjoyed the challenge and was over the moon to see that she was getting back into shape as quickly as she had hoped.

That fact alone kept the newspapers happy. The *Sunday People* tracked down the former timber mill in London's East End, where the new video was being filmed, and snatched photographs of slim-again Jade rehearsing in the American cheerleader-style miniskirt, tight cropped top and boxing boots she would wear for much of the recording itself.

'I've managed to drop down two dress sizes since giving birth,' Jade said when she started publicising the new routines on the unimaginatively titled 'New Jade Dance Workout'. 'If I can do it so can you.' That final sentence was to be the key selling point on the cover of tape and DVD. It was a simple but effective message, once again making the most of Jade's reputation as an ordinary woman who struggles with her weight but manages to come out on top.

Once more the tape featured Jade at her relaxed and self-deprecating best. She laughed and joked with the dancers, and got cross with herself for missing the beat and messing up the steps a few times. Again the verdict from the critics and the public was mixed. 'Jade, bless her, does try to keep the tone light-hearted but there is not much instruction,' wrote a reviewer on the Amazon website before finishing off with the kind of playful dig that Jade was now very used to. 'This is good for a light aerobic workout with slight toning, and you can always sit back and watch the male dancers or laugh at Jade's boots.'

But once more Jade could afford to laugh off the sarcasm. The 'New Jade Dance Workout' wouldn't end up selling anything like the same amount as the original tape, but it was no flop. And when the royalties were added to those she had earned on the first tape, her total fitness earnings would soon top £100,000 and ultimately peak at just over £120,000.

Once more the money wasn't the main motivation for Jade, however. What mattered to her more was the fact that she had once again gone down from a size 16 to a size 12, due almost entirely to a good diet and plenty of dancing. With a bit of luck she had also helped a few other women do the same.

As a turbulent, high-profile 2003 ended, Jade found she was still in good company in the celebrity stakes. She was sandwiched at number two, between Jordan at number one and Britney Spears at number three, in the Madame Tussaud's Personality of the Year Awards. The fact that the actual poll was for 'Most Pointless Personality' hardly mattered. Jade's name was still big enough to draw in the crowds and keep her in the public eye.

Jade was also enjoying her chance to mix in superstar circles and to experience a lifestyle she could have only ever dreamed about as a low-paid dental nurse in Bermondsey. She was photographed attending film premières and opening nights, and was always happy to turn up and give other television shows a lift when the ratings demanded it. Hence, her decision to have her hair cut in an episode of reality show *The Salon*, and her appearance on Gordon Ramsey's *Hell's Kitchen*, where she was interviewed on camera by Jordan and added yet another Jade-ism to her hall of fame. 'I thought the warm salad said worm salad,' she admitted, though thankfully not in the hearing of the famously volatile Gordon Ramsey.

Jade's growing wealth was also giving her the chance to do something she had long since dreamed about: some serious shopping. London's ritzy Bond Street, home of designer stores, from Gucci and Prada to Louis Vuitton and Tiffany's, was fast turning into one of her favourite places. Jade, the poor girl from the wrong side of the tracks in Bermondsey, admits she now has so many pairs of shoes that she needs a new wardrobe built specially for them. And she confesses to a love of designer labels – once spending £800 on a pair of Christian Dior boots.

The paparazzi also spotted her shopping on Bond Street just after cashing her first cheques from the media when she bought a £1,500 Cartier watch, a Gucci purse, bag and ring, plus some Chanel earrings and a necklace. But while her choice of shops was changing, Jade herself remained as natural as ever. 'I don't need to look around for other men when I've got Jeff at home,' she said in the summer of 2003. 'But I was just shopping in Bond Street and couldn't stop staring at this guy because he looked so stylish and rich. It was only when I got back to my car that my driver told me it was Robbie Williams. I'm such a wally and he must have thought I was so rude because I was just gawping at him the whole time.' It is a far cry even from Jade's early days of fame, when her shopping trips had been a little more modest. She had been snapped buying a poncho in Marks & Spencer in Lakeside, and was mobbed by fellow shoppers in the down-market Primark store in the equally down-market Lewisham, South-East London. Not areas where you run much risk of seeing millionaire pop stars.

So, able to shop pretty much wherever and whenever she wanted by the start of 2004, it was little wonder that Jade was actually feeling pretty happy about the way her career was developing. Amazingly enough, she was even able to turn down some well-paid work. Would she go on *The Weakest Link*, for instance? 'No, I'd hate it. Anne Robinson would absolutely hammer me, absolutely batter me. And it would be pointless. I'd be on there for one round.' So how about *Who Wants To Be A Millionaire?* 'I wouldn't even get on the seat because I'd be so slow,' she admitted.

It was all a far cry from the early days when she had come out of the *Big Brother* house and most people had predicted that she would fade from public view in a matter of months. No one had thought she would have the character, the intelligence or the dedication to carve out a successful career in the media. But more than 18 months on and Jade was still in demand. The only problem was that she didn't know whether her next big decision was about to ruin everything.

The dilemma came courtesy of her potential role in a big new £4.7 million reality show to be screened on Channel 5. It was to be called *Back To Reality* and it looked ideally suited to Jade's career to date. But Jade knew that things weren't this simple. What if this was one reality show too many and fans decided they were no longer interested in what she had to say? She was worried that she might be written off as a one-trick pony and become a laughing stock if she did yet another fly-on-the-wall show. Jade, like many other people, had watched in horror as the media ganged up on television presenter Anthea Turner after she was wrongly accused of signing a sponsorship deal to eat a new chocolate bar in her wedding photographs. The attacks had been so strong that Anthea had almost completely disappeared from our television screens and was struggling to find any alternative work. 'I'm a much newer star so, if the media turns on me in a similar way, I will be even less likely than Anthea to ever recover,' thought Jade.

But after much agonising Jade decided she couldn't – and indeed shouldn't – say no to the *Back To Reality* producers. She would stay true to herself and take any criticism as it came. 'I think the reason I am still doing OK is because I've never got above myself,' she said with surprising maturity just before the show began. 'I don't think I'm too good for anything. Like with this. I didn't go, "Oh no, I'm not going back into a house. I've come too far." At the end of the day it was a reality-TV programme that got me where I am in the first place.'

But there were some last-minute nerves. 'I'm looking forward to it, as long as the crowds are not all shouting "Burn the Pig" and holding up terrible posters again. I don't want to have to move house when I get out,' she said, worried as ever about how the public would react to seeing her back on their screens in another hidden-camera show.

But as a new mum Jade was determined never to repeat her reality-TV antics of the past. 'My son is my future and I'm not going to do anything to embarrass him,' she said just before going into the West London property renamed Reality Mansions for the duration of the programme. 'So if people are expecting to see me get drunk and strip off again, they'll be disappointed.' Jade, she said, had changed. Her life was different and she had been forced, yet again, to grow up fast. 'When I was in the *Big Brother* house I was all over the place,' she admitted. 'I was living with my mum, I had a bad boyfriend, my life wasn't going anywhere. But this time I've got a lovely partner, I've got my baby, I've got my home. I've got everything so I'm not going to go in there and act like a doughnut.'

Jade had an extraordinarily glamorous new image to think about and protect as well.

As part of the pre-publicity for the show Channel 5 had decided to give her a complete makeover, and paid for a photo session with the legendary fashion and celebrity photographer David La Chapelle. The results went on billboards across the country. And they were stunning.

David was an early pupil of Andy Warhol and has since snapped almost every famous name worth knowing. His most celebrated works include shots of Elton John metal detecting on a beach, an oiled-up and half-naked David Beckham, Puff Daddy draped over a gold-painted girl, Britney Spears in hot pants in her toy-filled bedroom, and Madonna dressed up like a goddess. The list of superstars goes on, and in 2004 Jade Goody's name was to be added to it. It was an extraordinary coup for a girl from Bermondsey who had been entirely unknown less than two years earlier.

Little wonder, then, that the day of the shoot was one of the most frightening of her life. Jade confessed to friends that she was terrified that someone like David La Chapelle would just focus on her flaws and wish he was with his usual, more famous and perfect clients. As it turned out, he didn't. He proved to have a fantastic sense of humour and soon had Jade confident enough to laugh along with him as they worked out what would look good on camera.

The scenario they finally came up with for the shots was typically David La Chapelle. And typically Jade Goody. She was dressed up to the nines in a light, sexy, pale-green dress, long straight hair falling over her face, a big white smile running across it. She was also holding chopsticks and eating noodles while surrounded by three muscular men in their underwear who were posing as paparazzi. It was as surreal and humorous as any of La Chapelle's other celebrity pictures. And it stands alone as worthy of show alongside any of them.

Jade, of course, was thrilled, and has a copy of the best shot on the wall at home in Essex. Next stop, David Bailey, she thought, as her most famous photographer to date packed up his cameras, kissed her goodbye and left the studio. With the pictures taken and the poster sites booked there was no backing out of the show. So, on her best behaviour, Jade entered Reality Mansion in Acton, West London, on Sunday, 15 February 2004.

All the contestants were in the show on behalf of their

chosen charities – the winner would see the prize fund of £75,000 given to the good cause or causes of their choice. New mum Jade had picked three charities. If she won the prize she wanted a third of the money to go to Tommy's, the charity that supports people who suffer from the problems of premature birth, miscarriages and stillbirth. Another third was to go to Scope, which helps people with cerebral palsy, and the final slice was earmarked for NCH, the children's charity that offers help and support to disadvantaged and vulnerable youngsters including young carers.

Just under two million people were watching as Jade joined her fellow contestants in the house. They were: Rik Waller from *Pop Idol*; Princess Diana's love-rat James Hewitt; two other names from *Big Brother*, Series 1 winner Craig Phillips and 'nasty' Nick Bateman; Ricardo Ribeiro from *The Salon*; television presenter and *Merseybeat* actress Josie D'Arby; Welsh pensioner Maureen Rees from *Driving School*; the American star of *Joe Millionaire*, Sarah Kozer; *Wife Swap*'s Lizzie Bardsley; spoon-bender and Michael Jackson pal Uri Geller; plus model and former *I'm A Celebrity – Get Me Out of Here* contestant Catalina Guirado.

In typically forthright fashion, Jade had said before going into the house that she wasn't looking forward to meeting Nick Bateman ('He's dodgy and he's got warts') or Rik Waller ('When I saw his video I thought, Urrrggghhhh because his teeth are yellow'). In a sweet and shy sort of way she hoped to make a friend out of James Hewitt, however. 'I thought he came across well on *The Games*,' she said, 'but I don't reckon he will like me. He'll think I'm an idiot and really common.'

In the end, Jade and James did get on well. But fewer people than expected were interested enough to watch. The show was on a minority channel, and was frequently scheduled against such tough competition as *Coronation Street* and *EastEnders* so it rarely enjoyed viewing figures of more than two million. To make matters worse, its time slot was changed frequently throughout the run to try and grab the best audience figures, and this ended up alienating many former fans, who gave up trying to guess when the next instalment was going to be transmitted.

The top brass at Channel 5 put a brave face on it, however. Programming director Dan Chambers said the show had been a success, even though viewing figures had been lower than expected. '*Back To Reality* may not have achieved the overall audiences we might have hoped for but it did deliver us the enormously attractive 16- to 34-year-old demographic in larger numbers than ever before and brought many people to the channel for the first time. I feel it was a very worthwhile thing,' he said.

One person Chambers could hardly have faulted when he analysed how the show had gone was Jade. She single-handedly kept the programme alive and in the public eye. Towards the end of the first of the three weeks that the guests lived in the Reality Mansion, Jade had one of her infamous and fantastically watchable tantrums, for example.

Big Rik Waller was her main target – and she reduced him to tears, many of which might have been genuine. The show's producers, so worried about the heated nature of the row, cut the live feed on the Internet for nearly an hour while the contestants calmed down. But Jade had ensured that the programme finally made it into the headlines.

A good selection of what are now called Jade-isms also kept reporters happy. 'I haven't any Tic Tacs to win this show,' she said at one point. Then there was: 'Is Jerusalem a real place? I thought it was just in the Bible.' 'Can't you drive to Ireland? I thought it was near Scotland so you must be able to drive there.' 'The potting shed. Is that where they smoke pot?' Then, perhaps the most worrying thought of all for some of her fellow contestants: 'If you chopped off my head I'd still carry on talking, because the head stays alive for a bit. I've seen that in films.'

Jade was centre stage again on Day 12 when a mystery guest came into the house. It was her boyfriend Jeff Brazier. Viewers and contestants raged about whether it was fair to give one competitor a genuinely friendly shoulder to cry on during the show. But the show's biggest moment was still to come. It was one o'clock in the morning on Day 14 when James Hewitt discovered Jade slumped on the floor of the mansion's bathroom. Yelling for help, he demanded that the producers call for an ambulance, and Jade was rushed off the set and taken to Central Middlesex Hospital for tests. Boyfriend Jeff, who was being interviewed by show host Richard Bacon at the time, rushed off the set and joined her in the ambulance as it rushed through the empty streets to the accident and emergency department.

Doctors carried out a series of tests and scans, and said Jade would have to stay in overnight while they waited for all the results. 'Jade is fairly comfortable and she is adamant she will return to the show,' said a Channel 5 spokesperson who sat with her after she had regained consciousness.

In her hospital bed Jade was terrified. Internet chat rooms had been abuzz with rumours that she was expecting a baby ever since the first few days of this latest show when she refused booze and asked if massages were safe for expectant mothers. While Jade was pretty sure that the rumours were right, she knew it was far too early to confirm them. For a start she hadn't yet had the vital 12-week scan, before which very few expectant mothers tell the world what is happening. To make matters even more complicated, Jade's mum Jackiey had gone to India on holiday just before *Back To Reality* had begun filming and Jade didn't want to tell the world her good news before telling her mum.

And had she lost the baby anyway? The wave of sickness that had overwhelmed her on the television set was stronger than any she had felt when she had been pregnant with Bobby Jack. Her collapse had been completely genuine – and she had effectively slipped in and out of consciousness during her ambulance ride to hospital, desperately trying to block out what was happening to her in a bid to conserve her strength. Being surrounded by doctors and undergoing a series of tests was only serving to increase Jade's worries. Maybe there was something else wrong with her, something completely unconnected to her possible pregnancy. She thought of Bobby and swore she would survive anything in order to give him the safe, secure upbringing that had been denied to her.

After a series of agonising delays hospital staff gave Jade

the all-clear and the doctors said that she was free to go back into Reality Mansions if she wanted. True to form, Jade decided that the show had to go on. 'She's a fighter, is our Jade,' said a proud Jeff, as she headed back to the set, greeted her fellow contestants with hugs, and laughed off her emergency illness as something triggered by James's awful cooking.

In the coming days, Jade was to talk more about the tests she had undergone, including examinations to see if she was suffering from a burst ovarian cyst. Without having seen her mum face to face, and without having had her routine scans, Jade decided she would be tempting fate to discuss her supposed pregnancy. So for once the potential mum vowed to keep mum.

Anyway, back in Reality Mansions, Jade looked in a strong position to win the show. The other housemates were rallying round her and Ladbrokes made her favourite to come out on top. 'We had no choice but to make her the favourite,' said spokesman Warren Lush. 'We underestimated her before and nearly lost a fortune,' he continued, referring back to the *Big Brother* days when bookies had to pay out big money on long odds of her staying in the house for more than a week.

In the event, though, Jade didn't win. She left the house after 20 long days in fourth position – the same result she achieved in *Big Brother*. The official *Back To Reality* champion turned out to be James Hewitt, who donated his £75,000 prize fund to the London-based homeless charity The Passage.

However, the extraordinary amount of publicity that

Jade had generated over the past month meant that she was once more the real winner of the show. And this was to be just the beginning of a whole new volatile chapter in her life. She was soon to feature in another unprecedented run of tabloid news stories and magazine covers. Her second baby was going to be big news. Her growing personal fortune would be an even bigger story. And her relationship with Jeff was about to hit the rocks.

chapter 12

Hello, Freddie

If she had been left alone then Jade's second pregnancy might have been a whole lot calmer than her first. She had tried desperately to learn the lessons from last time, when her mood swings and cravings had triggered massive rows between her and Jeff. This time, she said, she would be ready for the worst. She would be able to recognise the early warning signs and do something about them before the tension spilled over into yet another pointless argument.

Neither Jade nor Jeff had planned on having a second baby so soon after Bobby's arrival. But they were both enjoying being parents far more than they had expected and at some point they had always wanted a brother or sister for their young son. So, once the shock of Jade's second surprise pregnancy had passed, they started looking forward to an exciting, happy few months as 2004 got under way.

Unfortunately, the couple's high public profile meant that there always seemed to be someone just round the corner trying to cause trouble. And in the middle of March Jade started to get some terrible late-night phone calls. 'Jeff is having an affair,' a voice would say, and hang up. Or 'Jeff's cheating on you.' 'Jeff's seeing another woman while you're stuck at home.' Or 'You should find out what Jeff is getting up to when you're not around.'

At first Jade ignored the calls. She didn't recognise the voice on the other end of the line and as the callers had withheld their numbers she was unable to return the calls to find out any more. Jade tried to tell herself that it was just a stupid, cruel trick played by someone who didn't even have the courage to make an accusation to her face. It was the price of fame, she thought, and she would just have to grin and bear it.

But then Jade noticed that Jeff's phone started ringing late at night as well – and that he often left the room to take the calls. So could her anonymous caller be telling the truth and was Jeff having an affair? Jade was overcome with doubts. Jeff was a great partner, a fantastic father to Bobby and, despite all their rows, he always made her smile and she was still deeply in love with him. But could she trust him?

After a series of tearful discussions with her mum Jade decided to give Jeff the benefit of the doubt. But another bombshell was about to be dropped. A so-called Jade lookalike suddenly sold her story to the *People* and claimed that she had had passionate sex not once but twice with Jeff. The incidents had happened a year ago –

when Jade had been pregnant with Bobby. But the 19-year-old drama student was ready to give plenty of details of how Jeff had allegedly picked her up in an Essex nightclub to kick-start the affair. And Jade's confidence in her partner crumbled.

Angry and insecure Jade was also exhausted. Baby Bobby was thriving, but he had suffered several major attacks of croup – fierce coughing that can almost stop babies from breathing. Jade and Jeff had watched in terror as Bobby had suffered the first of them. In the worst cases babies' lips can literally go blue from lack of oxygen and it is incredibly hard to predict when the attacks will either begin or end. Bobby had needed hospital checks several times over the past few months, including an emergency visit to hospital on Boxing Day. While trying to stay calm, Jade was always frightened that another attack could be triggered at any moment.

She was also trying to help out at the couple's tanning salon and keep her media career on the rails after her recent role in the *Back To Reality* show. It was all getting too much and Jade's belief that she and Jeff could survive her second pregnancy without any major rows was soon to be shattered. Over the weeks their arguments became ever more frequent and ever more personal. Jeff always denied that he was having any sort of affair and blamed the newspapers for trying to spread false rumours. But Jade had no idea whether or not to believe him. Her stress levels were high, her hormones kicked in and the stage was set for the couple's biggest and most high-profile bust-up to date.

It all began one evening when Jeff headed out to the E10 bar in nearby Leyton with 13 work colleagues – only three of them men. An embarrassed Jade now admits that she lost control and started to ring him repeatedly on his mobile phone to find out exactly where he was, who he was with and what he was doing. And, however irrational it was, she froze to her core when one of Jeff's female colleagues answered the phone.

Jade spent the next few hours at home worrying, working herself up into a frenzy and crying. And when Jeff returned home at 2 a.m. she was ready for a fight. No one knows exactly what happened – though almost every newspaper would carry its own version of events over the next few days. What we do know is that accusations started to fly the moment Jeff got through the front door.

One set of claims says he raised his fist to Jade – though both he and Jade soon went into print to deny it. Lurid stories also hit the headlines saying that Jade had dived for the knife drawer at their home and had hit Jeff dozens of times as he tried to stop her from opening it. What we also know for certain is that Jade's mum Jackiey was so scared that the fight had got out of control that she dialled 999 from the first floor of the house while cradling a crying baby Bobby in her arms.

Jeff then fled the house in his car and headed to the nearby home of his aunt, who said he should go to hospital to have the bruises and scratches on his face and arms checked out by doctors. On the way back from the A & E department Jeff was told that the police wanted to speak to him so he handed himself in at the local police station and was held in the cells for eight hours while they did the paperwork on the case. The confusion over events meant that Jade was also arrested for assault, so she could give her side of the story – and answer the claims made by Jeff in his statement.

Jade later said that it had been a terrible, humiliating experience, and, while neither she nor Jeff were charged with any offences, they had both been horrified at the prospect of getting a police record just because their passions had got out of control. And this wasn't actually the first time the couple's arguments had got them into trouble with the law. The previous July the police had found them both rowing uncontrollably in a lay-by in Essex in the early hours of the morning. On that occasion they had both been arrested for suspected drink-driving, and as there was no evidence of exactly who had been behind the wheel they were taken to the police station for second breath tests, which found they were both under the limit.

At that point the couple's relationship seemed to have stretched past its breaking point. Unable to see a future for them, Jeff had moved out of their home for three days, turning off his phone and refusing to say where he was going or what he planned to do. That experience had been an extraordinary wake-up call for Jade, then just 22. She had suddenly seen herself alone, a single parent, repeating all the patterns of her past. More importantly, she had realised that she did still love Jeff and wanted to be with him more than any other man she had ever met. But had she blown it? Was there any way to salvage the situation and build a better, stronger foundation for the future?

'I don't know where Jeff is. I've tried to call him but I've heard nothing. We had a huge row and I said some things I shouldn't. I've been in tears ever since. I really miss him and I can't believe it's over. I say things without thinking but don't always mean them. I still love Jeff and want him back,' Jade told a friend back then as she asked everyone who knew Jeff to tell him to come home.

Alone, worried and left to think about what she really needed, Jade recognised that, more than anything, she wanted Jeff to be in her life and a full-time dad to their baby. She wanted to be part of a stable, two-parent family she and Jeff had both missed out on in their own childhoods. But she thought she had driven Jeff away for good. In desperation she took her friend's advice and put her thoughts down on paper in a sealed note to Jeff. Not knowing if it would ever be read, she left the envelope on the kitchen table, hoping he might find it if he broke cover and came round one day while she was out. Luckily for them both – and for their baby son – Jeff did just that. He found the note and it did the trick.

'It was beautiful,' he said after reading it and admitting that it had moved him to tears. 'It was every reassurance I ever needed. She didn't like being without me and since then it has been perfect. It's like we started again. I can see the love and the effort.'

So the couple had given their relationship a second try. But, despite all their efforts, they never seemed able to build any really firm foundations for the future, and less than a year later it looked as if their second big separation would be more permanent. Jeff had taken all his possessions to his aunt's Hertfordshire pub after their most recent late-night row and it looked as if Jade's fairy-tale relationship was all over.

'This is definitely the end for Jade and Jeff,' said mum Jackiey as she tried to help Jade come to terms with life on her own. But, while Jade knew that she could easily support herself and her growing family, she wasn't so sure that she wanted her children to live without a stable father figure. So an uneasy truce developed between the ex-lovers. Their relationship appeared to be over for good. But Jeff started house-hunting so he could live within a few streets of his former partner.

More urgently, the warring couple had to work out how they could possibly handle the imminent birth of their second child. Jade admits she didn't know if she could face having Jeff in the maternity room with her. 'I'm not sure if I would feel comfortable with Jeff being there,' she told *OK!* magazine in an exclusive interview just before the birth, as public interest in Jade's troubled life hit a new high. 'You need support, you need somebody there to go, "I love you." And I don't know if that's going to happen with me and Jeff. It's a very awkward situation and I'm pretty confused about it.'

But the clock was ticking, and decisions had to be made pretty soon. Jade decided a change of scene might help her decide what to do next. So she, baby Bobby, a friend and her baby son went to the Canary Islands for a few days. But disaster very nearly struck when Jade took a swim in the hotel pool. Suddenly she felt some dreadful pains and was convinced her waters had broken. It was improbably early for this to have happened, but as Bobby had been born four weeks premature, Jade wasn't taking any chances.

Hotel staff called an ambulance and she was taken to a hospital on the tiny island, where very few staff spoke English. 'It was so scary and the doctors managed to tell me that they thought the baby wanted to come out, but this was two months early. The only thing the doctor could say to me was, "If this baby comes out your life is in danger, the baby's life is in danger and we will have to fly you to Gran Canaria as we don't have the facilities here."'

Jade broke down in tears. 'Jeff wasn't there and my friend was looking after Bobby and her son back at the hotel,' she says. 'I was there all on my own, sobbing my heart out. It was an awful experience. They started giving me drugs and I was trying to tell them that I was allergic to penicillin and plasters. They stuck a plaster on my hand and I thought, I'm going to die.'

By good luck, the local Spanish doctors were able to stabilise Jade's position, and back in Britain doctors said that, while her waters had indeed broken two months early, they had since managed to build back up again. Jade spent the next few weeks going in and out of hospital, including one particularly frightening seven-night stay when she went into mini labour and had to have the contractions artificially halted to ensure her baby wouldn't be harmed by being born too soon.

And amid all the pain and worry one bright light began to shine. Jeff was back on the scene. Not as a partner or a lover, but as a good friend. 'He was very supportive,' Jade said. 'In fact, he was more supportive than I thought he was going to be. It was at that point that I decided he should be at the birth. When I was in pain he stayed at the hospital with me. He was really good.'

But when would the birth be? After so many weeks of health scares the doctors finally had some good news for Jade in the middle of September. They said that she was over the worst, that her waters had fully built up again and that she was going to go to full term. Everyone relaxed, Jade went home and life went back to normal. But the doctors turned out to be wrong.

It was midnight on 17 September, almost exactly a month before Jade's due date, when a series of sharp pains woke her up in bed. She turned on the lights, tried to breathe slowly and work out how serious it might be. Then she saw blood on the sheets. It was serious.

She dragged herself to the bathroom, screaming for mum Jackiey to help. Between them they called an ambulance, and Jeff, who was more than 50 miles away in Colchester to help celebrate his brother's birthday. Jade began to panic as the minutes passed and no ambulance arrived. But a local hero did suddenly turn up in its place – Lee Howells, who is Bobby Jack's godfather and Jeff's best friend. Desperately worried and feeling powerless in Colchester, Jeff had called his pal and asked him to rush round to see if he could help. Having never been so pleased to see anyone in her life, Jade gave up on the

ambulance and got into Lee's car. But disaster was about
to strike once more because Lee didn't know the area well
enough to find his way to the hospital.

'I was in the back of Lee's car on all fours screaming and
every time we went over a speed bump the pain felt so
awful. Poor Lee! I looked up and noticed we were going in
the totally wrong direction for the hospital,' said Jade.
'And by the time we did get there, all the doors were
locked, so Lee was banging on the doors trying to get help.'

Mercifully, the pair did find the right way into the
hospital in the end, and Jade was whisked to the maternity
unit at Harlow's Princess Alexandra Hospital while Jeff
was motoring down the A12 from north Essex to try and
be there in time for the birth. On his arrival, he and Jade's
mum didn't end up waiting very long. Jade's actual labour
was fast, especially compared with last time, when baby
Bobby took nine long hours to appear. But there were
problems immediately after her second birth – both for
mum and newborn son Freddy.

The first thing that happened was that the midwives and
doctors spotted Jade was bleeding after the birth – and
nothing they could do would stop it. After further
investigations they realised that she would need an
emergency operation – so, with Freddy in the arms of the
nurses, Jade was wheeled down to the operating theatre
for surgery. She came round over an hour later while being
given an emergency blood transfusion. 'I was being given
four pints of blood as I was losing so much of it,' she said,
after having been told that the cause of the crisis was
actually very minor. 'I had this little paper cut which was

making me bleed. It's hard to think that it was so traumatic but in the end they just stitched me up and it was fine. However, this meant I didn't get to see Freddy for the first day. I was so white and had gone anaemic.'

Meanwhile, Freddy himself had started some warning bells ringing. The boy weighed a relatively healthy 6 lb 6 oz but was still considered too weak to be taken out of the Special Care Baby Unit, where he had been placed during Jade's surgery. So he stayed in his incubator alongside all the other premature babies in the hospital for the next nine days.

Like any new mum, Jade was heartbroken that she couldn't hold her new baby in bed, let along take him home with her. 'Leaving him in hospital was hard. I thought it might have been easier because I'd done it with Bobby, but it was tough. I was literally sobbing when I had to leave him,' she said afterwards. As she had decided to breastfeed, Jade had to be in and out of the hospital every few hours before Freddy was finally given the all-clear and she was able to take him home to live with her and his big brother Bobby.

As if this awful fortnight hadn't been bad enough, Jeff hadn't been able to stay around to help. After rushing down to Harlow for the birth, he had been forced to leave to take part in his latest reality-TV project, *The Farm*, which he went on to win. Fortunately, while Jeff had been in the hospital, he and Jade were able to put all their past differences aside and focus on their children. 'They seemed to be getting on very well,' said one fellow mum in the Essex hospital. 'Jeff was holding Jade's hand and looking after her like any new father would do. It was all very emotional, really touching, and Jade and Jeff couldn't stop smiling. Their son is really cute and it was obvious that they were both delighted.'

The couple were not, however, ready to live together again. After so many close calls, false alarms and sudden reconciliations, it looked as if the Jade and Jeff romance was finally over. Separate lives loomed. And Jade realised that she herself had turned into a single mother.

'I know that Jeff will help but for most of the time I'll be on my own,' she admitted, trying to put a brave face on things two months after Freddy was born. 'Loading the car this morning took me about an hour. But I've got friends and my mum has been absolutely amazing, and all Jeff's friends have been supportive and helped me out. I know that sooner or later that will die down and I'll be a single mum and it won't be easy.'

Single mum or not, Jade was certainly inspiring other mums with the clear love of her two boys. 'I won't put up with cheekiness or bad manners – I'm pretty strict,' she had admitted. So it was little surprise that she made the top three in the 2004 Quality Street Mum of the Year Competition – Ulrike Jonsson came first. It was rare for Jade to get public praise like this for the way she was running her life and her family. But, just in case this sort of unsolicited compliment went to her head, Jade was then told about a slightly different parental poll. At fourth position, she was only one place behind Michael Jackson in the list of the World's Most Embarrassing Parents compiled by TV company Trouble. So, as ever, Jade continued to get mixed reviews and divide the nation. To make matters worse, there was the financial side of her relationship with Jeff to sort out as well. And it appeared that there was a huge amount of money at stake.

At the start of 2004 it had been reported that Jade had passed an amazing milestone. At just 22 years old, and little more than 18 months after first exploding on to the nation's television screens in *Big Brother*, Jade Goody was revealed to be Britain's first reality-TV millionaire.

The belated royalties she had just received from the fitness videos and DVDs she had made in 2002 easily pushed her other earnings past the magic million-pound mark. As her estranged father Andy said, 'People called her thick but they underestimated her. She's done it against all the odds. I bet those who called her dumb are laughing on the other side of their faces now.'

Jade, it appeared, had been laughing all the way to the bank for the past two years. Figures are notoriously hard to confirm, but entertainment experts said Jade's big-money deals had begun the moment she left the *Big Brother* house and had actually been increasing ever since. The analysts said that in less than two years she had made more than £690,000 from newspaper and magazine interviews, serialisations and photo shoots, another £120,000 from her panto in Kent and television shows including *Celebrity Driving School* and *What Jade Did Next*, a staggering £100,000 from her extensive series of personal appearances across the country, and nearly £130,000 from her dance videos and spin-offs. That money dwarfed the rewards paid to all the other former

Big Brother housemates, as the following chapters reveal. And it seemed that Jade had been investing it more sensibly than most people might have thought. Buying property as soon as she had been able to afford it had certainly turned out to be a smart move – house prices have risen dramatically since she first bought in 2003.

Toby Walne from the *Mail on Sunday* comments, 'Jade's long-term future is also more assured because she has made so much so young. It is an obvious cliché, but the sooner you start putting some money aside, the longer it has to grow. That's why old money is almost always big money. If Jade invests in property and other assets in her early twenties, then she's likely to have a real nest egg to look forward to in her forties and beyond. She has done incredibly well so far and it looks like she's made plenty of good financial decisions.'

Other show-business experts agreed that the financial future was particularly bright for Jade. 'It's the next couple of years where the big money is to be made. Jade has served her apprenticeship but it is only now that sponsors and advertisers will really start to take notice,' said Max Clifford, who had correctly predicted that Jade would earn her first million within a year of leaving the *Big Brother* house.

With this much money at stake, it was little wonder that Jade didn't want to destroy everything and risk losing half her gains in an expensive bust-up with Jeff. The pair had never been married, so a standard divorce-style settlement wasn't on the cards. But Jeff did apparently feel he was entitled to some of Jade's wealth. 'Essex wars' screamed one paper's headline in a feature on celebrity bust-ups that also included details of J-Lo's divorce from Ben Affleck and the impending split between former Westlife star Brian McFadden and *I'm A Celebrity – Get Me Out Of Here* winner Kerry Katona.

At one point the papers said Jeff wanted half the value of the three-storey Essex home they used to share, complete ownership of their thriving local sunbed shop, plus the top-of-the-range £40,000 Mercedes that Jade bought before she had even passed her driving test. Anonymous 'friends' were quoted as saying that Jeff had only ever dated Jade to boost his own faltering career as a television presenter – so she had already given him enough financial and career help, and no longer owed him a penny. Other 'sources' said that Jade hadn't invested much, or worked very hard, on the sunbed business, so she couldn't now claim any ownership of its assets or future profits.

What we do know for sure is that lawyers were called – by both sides in the dispute. 'We've both gone to lawyers over money,' said Jade towards the end of 2004 when their latest break-up was still hot news. 'When I met Jeff, he was a builder. I was the one who was earning and I think that caused a lot of problems because I don't think men like it when their partner earns more than they do.' As her close family can attest, Jade has always been prepared to share her good fortune, however. 'I was never mean with money,' she said, before showing a touch of unexpected steel. 'When Jeff and I were together whatever I had was shared with him, but now we're not together that doesn't stand and I'm not going to roll over on that.'

Thankfully, Jade and Jeff had never forgotten the two entirely innocent potential victims in their latest break-up – Bobby and Freddy. So when they realised that they were likely to split for good, and that there were big financial and other implications, they decided to let the experts take control, allowing them to focus on being good parents. 'This makes it easier because we don't have to have the rows over money. We can leave that to our lawyers. We still talk and have a laugh together.' Jade was also determined to shut the door firmly on one other shadow from the past that she feared could seriously threaten her family's well-being: the potential influence of her estranged father Andy.

Despite being frozen out of Jade's life a year ago, he decided that the birth of her second child could give him a fresh start. 'I want to go straight and be the perfect grandfather,' he told reporters from his latest prison cell. 'Seeing Jade blossom despite all the hardship has made me realise that there is no excuse for what I've done. I know I have been a bad father – now I can make it up by being a good grandfather.'

But Jade was horrified at the prospect. Andy had been taken back to jail the previous year after yet another drug-related conviction – it was estimated to be his 50th conviction in total, spread over more than 25 years. And Jade didn't want any part of that world threatening her new family. 'I don't take drugs, Jeff doesn't take drugs, none of our friends take drugs. Why would I bring my father into my children's lives when he could be a bad influence?' she said.

When all this heat was on at home, however, Jade turned to the one other development in her life that kept her sane: work.

If Bobby and Freddy had to grow up in a one-parent household like she had, then at least they would have financial security, she reasoned. At least they would be able to have all the physical things and the educational advantages she had lacked. 'All the money I earn is going to help my kids have a better life. I want to be able to give them as much as I can,' she said. There were reports that the girl who had left school with precious few qualifications was putting her babies' names on the list for the posh and private £2,335-a-term Heath Mount School near Hertford, where she hoped they would be guaranteed a five-star education. It's where Victoria Beckham had allegedly enrolled Brooklyn. But, after admitting she had visited the private school, Jade said she hadn't yet made any firm plans about her children's education.

And whatever she decided for them, there was money to be earned first. Despite the tensions between her and Jeff over the value and ownership of the sunbed shop in South Woodford, Jade was determined to carry on focusing on the beauty business. So out of the limelight she carried on racking up relevant qualifications to help her gain even more credibility in that world. 'I've now taken courses and got certificates for waxing and facials,' she said proudly. 'I love doing the facials and all the beauty side. I've also just passed my test in Brazilian waxing and St Tropez fake tanning.' But Jade admitted that she might just focus on the latter if she does ever set up her own business. 'I hate doing Brazilian waxing, though. It's just too much information,' she admits.

In her other, more public life, Jade had signed one lucrative deal just before Freddy had been born – to be the *Big Brother* correspondent of *OK!* magazine and write a weekly commentary on the fifth series. This began at the end of May 2004 and was about to introduce the likes of Nadia, Shell, Michelle, Stuart, Ahmed, Dan and Jason to the world.

Sticking to the reality-TV theme, in November Jade also signed up to be the *I'm A Celebrity – Get Me Out Of Here!* expert on old pal Paul O'Grady's new ITV chat show. 'Jade's sitting at home every night watching everything that happens in the jungle so we don't have to,' Paul said on her first appearance.

'Yeah, it says a lot about my social life,' she replied with a laugh.

But at least the short-term gig eased her back on to mainstream television after an earlier appearance on *This Morning* just after Freddy's birth, when she had told viewers about her massive blood loss and prompted one *Sun* reader to write to the paper saying she still looked fantastic. Far less flattering comments posted on Internet chat sites around this time showed that many people still laughed at and disliked Jade Goody. But many, many more had clearly taken her to their hearts.

'She went from public enemy number one to national treasure in the space of a few months,' said *Daily Star* reporter Simon Button in early 2004. And her fame has lasted. As 2004 drew to a close she was one of just nine celebrities asked to send Christmas messages to readers of

Heat magazine – the others included the Osbournes, Simon Cowell and Ricky Gervais. And Jade had one more big role to play before the year was out.

Jade was to be the foundation stone of Channel 4's unique *Big Brother Panto* show, which began broadcasting on digital channel E4 on 20 December and was repeated with a daily one-hour live extracts and highlights show on Channel 4 for the next three weeks.

From the start, Jade was always going to be the star of the show. She was the first face to be shown in its opening credits, the first person to be taken into the house on Day 1 and the first to enter its tiny Diary Room to record her thoughts on the experience and on her fellow housemates. Jade was also the only housemate whose face appeared on the cover of any of the magazines being advertised in the show's commercial breaks.

More controversially, Jade was also estimated to be earning a staggering four times the amount paid to the other *Big Brother* housemates for their parts in the same show – and the new panto was the ultimate proof that her earnings were rising, not falling, as time went by. In 2002 she had hit the headlines for being paid what was then a record £20,000 for appearing in panto in Gravesend, Kent, for example. But in 2004 her pay day for agreeing to be in the *Big Brother Panto* was worth half as much again – an extraordinary £30,000. The other nine *Big Brother* stars were said to be earning just £5,000 each for the same 17-day gig – and there were rumours that several wanted to go on strike when they heard how differently Jade was being treated in the pay stakes.

On the money front, former medical saleswoman Narinder, who had hogged the headlines in *Big Brother 2* a year before Jade found fame, was typical of the rest of the show's former contestants. In December 2004, as *Big Brother Panto* was preparing to air, *Heat* magazine asked the 32-year-old if she still made money out of being 'Narinder from *Big Brother*'. 'Oh God, no. I've been completely and utterly skint,' she replied honestly. 'I've done bits and bobs but it doesn't pay the mortgage.'

'Jade's left us Z-listers behind,' added PJ Ellis, with whom Jade had so famously shared a bed and possibly more on camera two years earlier, and who had hardly been seen since.

The premise behind *Big Brother Panto* was simple: starting from scratch the 10 housemates had to cast, learn and rehearse an all-singing, all-dancing pantomime. They would then have to perform it on live television at the end of the series. Top writers, acting coaches, dance choreographers and other experts were to come in every day to help everyone's performances as viewers watched how each of them rose to, or failed, the various challenges.

Jade actually found things difficult during the first few days in the house, which had been designed to look like a mountain lodge complete with outdoor hot tub and a big roaring fire. She was missing her two children, and other strong personalities dominated the early conversations, with Victor, Mel and Marco all making more noise than her. Even the notoriously grumpy Kitten was proving to be more central to the initial group dynamic on the show.

But, for all her reticence, Jade was still a woman with a

mission. She wanted the lead role of Cinderella and it is easy to see why. The bullied, abused underdog who finally turns into a star. It was a role Jade was born to play. 'I've been down that road before,' she said when the producers suggested she should audition as one of the ugly sisters instead. 'I've never been a princess, I just want to be someone pretty for a change,' she begged once more when the panto producers finally narrowed down the competition for this plum role to just Jade and Anouska from *Big Brother 4*.

In the end, both had to perform a short scene in front of a panel of judges before the decision was given to a public phone vote. Jade smiled broadly but didn't say a word when it was announced that she had won – with a staggering 83 per cent of the public poll.

'I wanted to go "Yeah!" but I thought I shouldn't,' she admitted to old pal Spencer after hearing the news. And after giving Anouska a hug she was ready with another joke at her own expense. 'You'd better work on your biceps because you've got to lift me up now,' she told the boys who might have preferred a dance routine with a slightly slimmer and lighter Cinderella. Of course, even now the newspapers couldn't resist gently mocking Jade. The *Independent*, when light-heartedly casting a fantasy celebrity pantomime, reckoned it had found the perfect role for Jade. But it wasn't Cinderella. It wasn't even an ugly sister. It was as 'the Christmas pudding'.

Back in the panto house, getting the lead role was actually a bigger relief than Jade was letting on, because she was already feeling under slightly more pressure than the other members of the mocked-up mountain lodge where they were living. The reason? As to be expected with Jade, it was her personal life. As well as T4's June Sarpong, the producers were planning to bring on Jade's estranged partner Jeff Brazier to co-host some of the highlights shows and to interview the panto housemates. It meant the father of her two children was potentially going to be commenting on her every move in the house, and quizzing her about her feelings. He was going to be introducing the live show itself on 5 January – and he would be watching from the stalls. It is the sort of scrutiny that would make anyone nervous. And Jade was no exception.

In the meantime, there was plenty of work to be done. Chris Denys, principal of the prestigious Bristol Old Vic Theatre School, had been brought in to direct the panto and from the start he said he thought he would have his work cut out for him. The housemates were working from a hastily written comic script by celebrated author Jonathan Harvey whose previous credits included *Gimme Gimme Gimme* and *Beautiful Thing*. The chief choreographer was Louie Spence, who has worked with pop stars Kylie, Mis-teeq and the Spice Girls, as well as helping create the moves on former *EastEnders* star Patsy Palmer's 'Ibiza Workout' video. Finally, *Faking It*'s Dave Lynn was there to teach the boys how to dress and move as girls, as well as advising everyone on how to project their personalities beyond the footlights in the theatre that was being specially built for this unique, one-off performance.

It was a full-on experience for everyone in the panto house, and tensions soon started to mount. Jade and Kitten had one of the biggest rows in the house when the animal-rights and human-rights activist complained about her role and walked out of some early rehearsals. As ever, we would also get to hear some great new Jade-isms as the show progressed. 'The housemates are on a rant-age, I think it's called,' she told the Diary Room. 'No, I mean they're on a volt.'

Meanwhile, the way Jade had single-handedly dominated public consciousness of all five series of *Big Brother* to date became apparent when the panto script was delivered. Famous Jade-isms littered the text and ultimately raised some great laughs from the audience. The panto was set in 'East Angular', the ugly sisters were described as 'minging', and when Jade's Cinderella decided to leave home she said, 'I'll head to the Cambridge River. Oh no, that's abroad, isn't it?' Then when Cinders finally tried on the glass slipper, 'nasty' Nick yelled out she shouldn't because of her verruca. The list could go on.

After just over two weeks of rehearsals, the panto housemates woke up and got ready to perform their live show on schedule. 'I dreamed that we forgot all our lines and that only two people turned up to watch us, Spencer's brother and my husband,' said Narinda during breakfast on the final morning.

'Dreams mean the opposite so it's going to be a success,' Jade replied.

And she was determined to make it one. Not least because Jeff was in the audience having been employed by

Channel 4 to interview the family and friends of the cast before the house lights dimmed and the performance began. His final interviews were with several of Jade's closest friends – then, right on cue, he announced the play was beginning and sat down to watch the action.

Big Brother Series 5 contestant Marco was first on stage. 'Our tale today is of rags to riches, of a lowly servant girl and right pair of...' he began with a wink, setting the tone for the type of humour to come.

As Cinderella, Jade was central to the action, taking part in three big dance routines as well as roller-skating round the stage and going through some fast costume changes. And at the end, as the crowd and her fellow actors applauded, Jade was the last person to take her bow.

The ratings for the show hadn't turned out to be that high, partly because Channel 4 had decided to put it on mid-morning every day rather than giving it a prime-time evening slot. Some strange editing – or lack of editing – meant that even in the highlights shows there were huge gaps in the soundtrack, where producers tried to drown out the words of housemates saying things deemed too rude or legally sensitive to be broadcast. These are the moments that are normally cut out of shows like *Big Brother* before they are transmitted because they are too boring to watch and disrupt the flow of the programme. For reasons that were never explained they stayed in during *Big Brother Panto*, in all likelihood persuading thousands of potential viewers to turn over or switch off.

But, as far as Jade was concerned, the show had been a success. 'I'd rather be at home with my kids, to be honest,' she had said in the first week when petty arguments between the housemates were starting to irritate everyone. But in reality she knew she had to stay. The instruction she had received had been top-notch, and was giving her even more confidence in her ability as an all-round entertainer. In particular, she was glad she had proved herself once more as a decent dancer and a strong live performer.

Big Brother Panto had been another important showcase for Jade's talents. And she was hoping it might lead to something big in the New Year.

chapter 13

Bye-Bye, Jeff

Despite the pressures of rehearsing for the Big Brother Panto, Jade was desperately looking forward to Christmas. She was having fun wrapping presents and dressing both Bobby and Freddy in cute Christmas outfits, often complete with reindeer horns and pictures of smiling, carrot-nosed snowmen.

Their house was full of bright, colourful decorations and she had put a life-size Father Christmas outside to make the garden look magical as well. Perhaps not everything was exactly right in her life, but Jade was determined to make it a Christmas to remember and wanted to put on a fantastic show for her children.

'Christmas is a very special time and I want it to be perfect for my boys,' she said. And that meant their dad had to be on hand throughout the holidays. Neither Jade nor Jeff liked the idea of having their children shuttle from one house to another at a time like Christmas. So Jeff headed back across town to stay in his old home for a few days – with a Santa suit in his bag to wear on the big day itself. Jade's mum Jackiey was also on hand, back in favour after a recent and highly public row with her daughter. So three generations would be under one roof to enjoy the holidays – pretty much a record for the fractured Goody family.

As it turned out, Jade's dreams of a perfect Christmas came true. Everyone got on well and the boys were overcome with excitement from the moment they woke up on Christmas Morning to the moment Jade fell asleep on Bobby's bed – still wearing her apron – after trying to tell them a bedtime story.

So even with the past few months' talk of a permanent split, could it still be happy families at last for Jade and Jeff? Jade was still holding out some hope of a fairy-tale ending to the biggest romance of her life. 'I'd love us to be like a proper family and it would be great for the boys if Jeff and I could live happily under the same roof. There's definitely something still there between us. Neither of us has shut the door completely and it would be perfect if it all worked out, but it's very complicated so we'll just have to wait and see what happens,' she said.

The pair had certainly staked their claim as one of Britain's best-known and most talked-about on-off couples. But, regardless of a seemingly endless stream of photo opportunities and occasional interviews, very little is actually known about the man in the middle of this most turbulent of relationships.

His career as a footballer never really took off, despite his gifts as an athlete. At Leyton Orient, Jeff was just one of the very many talented young men desperate to get noticed and get into the main team. But when just 11 men can go on the pitch at any one time an awful lot are left on the bench. Jeff, sad to say, was one of them.

Yet he wasn't entirely overlooked by the outside world. Blond and boyish, he was trying to boost his semi-professional's wage with some modelling – earning the nickname of 'pin-up Brazier' with his teammates. And, while big-time modelling jobs are few and far between for even the most handsome of men, Jeff did get some relatively regular work, and then set his sights on another potential career: television.

His first really big break was making it past nearly 20,000 other applicants to appear on the reality-TV show *Shipwrecked* in 2001. This was pitched as one of the 'worthier' reality shows – not basing its appeal entirely on competitions and evictions but instead trying to see which contestants fared best when trying to survive on a desert island.

Jeff was happy to admit that his motives for trying to get on the show were mixed, to say the least. 'If I am completely honest, I applied after I had been out to clubs with a mate who had been on the show and I saw that people would recognise him. It wasn't the fame that appealed to me, it was the respect that people gave him. He did really well on the show because he was just himself, and that's why he got a lot of love and appreciation afterwards.'

So Jeff followed his friend's lead, though he didn't himself win, or get particularly famous on the show. Immediately afterwards he was forced to go back into the building trade to help pay his bills. But he had loved being on *Shipwrecked* and had loved learning more about how television shows were made. At 22 years old he had been bitten by the media bug and was convinced he could make a living as a presenter.

Shortly afterwards, of course, he met Jade – then arguably the most famous young woman in Britain. So did he just date her to boost his own profile and kick-start his career? The cynics are not always prepared to give him the benefit of the doubt. When reviewing *The Farm* – which Jeff ultimately won – the *Scotsman*'s Grant Stott wrote, 'They keep introducing Jeff Brazier as "TV presenter Jeff Brazier". But has anyone ever seen anything he has presented? I thought not. Why not just say he's Jade Goody's ex?' Other critics constantly referred to Jeff as a 'gold-digger' for being with Jade.

In reality, Jeff had found regular television work by this stage of his career. And Jade, for one, was convinced he had won every job on merit. 'Jeff has got a great personality and good luck to him,' she said, as his workload grew alongside hers. 'He wasn't with me because of all that and, if anything, he would have been happy to walk away from it all.' At one point, she says, Jeff had actually suggested that the family leave Britain and start a new life in America.

Jeff had thought that he could have found television work there or gone back to his old role as a builder, while Jade could have become a stay-at-home mother or worked part-time as a beautician. But they never pursued the idea, mainly because Jade didn't want to go abroad and leave her mum on her own on this side of the Atlantic. She was also sure that, for the moment, they could both give their children a better future by staying in Britain and continuing to work in the media here.

For Jeff this meant a variety of new reality-TV shows and endurance games. He has now sweated his way though ITV's *Simply the Best*, where teams battle through a series of *It's A Knockout*-style challenges, and has featured in the likes of *I'm Famous and Frightened* on Living TV.

He was also a regular presenter on Channel 4's weekend morning shows – including T4's *Dirty Laundry*, which he co-hosted with fellow rising star and good friend June Sarpong. The live show included a host of studio and location interviews and interactions with viewers, so presenting it wasn't easy. 'I was a bit wooden at first but you can't be great at something straight away,' Jeff admitted. 'Simple things like reading the autocue wasn't something that came naturally, but I learned to relax and look like I'm not reading from something.' He was over the moon when he was asked back to co-present another series of the show in 2003. 'It's not a bad starting block so I am really grateful for it. The show gave me confidence, and now I've got my foot in the door I feel I can do it and I think I've done well.'

The bright and increasingly blond Jeff did have a lot going for him, not least the cheeky, cheerful manner that could endear him to the right type of audience. And, as his roster of live shows continues to grow, he has gained in confidence and professionalism. It may be some time before he can rival the likes of Dermot O'Leary or Ant and Dec. But he has managed to drag himself away from Jade's long shadow. He is also facing up to the challenges of a life spent at least partly in the public eye.

'I remember the days when I could go out with my mates and not worry about what anyone thought,' he said after his first few years in the limelight. 'Before I went on telly I could go into a club and no one would know me, and I was lively and I'd generally have a great time. But now I feel I have to tone myself down a bit.' It is a sacrifice he is prepared to make, though. 'I've got my career to think about. Things like going out aren't important in the long run,' he believes.

If Jeff's career was ever going to really take off, however, what he needed was a breakthrough role like *Big Brother* to sear him into the national consciousness. And in September 2004 he thought he might have found one.

Channel 5 had turned to *Big Brother* production company Endemol to come up with a similar but more constructive format. They, in turn, had come back with *The Farm* – a reality show billed as 'factual entertainment'. The idea was to put a group of media types, sports people and famous names on a working farm for three weeks. The contestants would live without electricity and running water, and would show viewers just how hard today's farmers have to work. And they would also put themselves up for eviction – just as in *Big Brother*. Jeff, however, was hoping he could survive all the cuts. 'I'm not overly confrontational, and perhaps it is big-headed of me to say it but I was sure people would like me,' he said afterwards.

But at the time it looked as if he would never get the chance to find out. He was getting ready for the first day alongside the likes of Stan Collymore, Vanilla Ice, Rebecca Loos, Paul Daniels and Debbie McGee when Jade went into premature labour with their second child. Even though the couple were estranged, Jade had finally decided that she wanted Jeff with her for the birth and he said he would happily have turned down any television role to join her. Fortunately, he didn't need to. The filming schedule meant he could see the arrival of little Freddy at the Princess Alexandra Hospital in Harlow while still joining the others at Richard Guy's East Hill View Farm in West Wiltshire.

The show was billed as *Big Brother*, but with a little more reality and a lot more relevance. And it was to prove controversial, to say the least. Jeff may have inseminated a pig – artificially, of course – but David Beckham's alleged lover Rebecca Loos went one step further and was filmed masturbating a different one to collect semen. The tabloids went wild, broadcasting watchdogs were swamped with complaints, and animal charities such as the RSPCA slammed it as 'both morbid and sordid'.

But viewing figures enjoyed a boost and stayed up for the rest of the series – when Jeff was crowned Top Farmer, narrowly beating American rap star Vanilla Ice in the final. 'I loved the experience. I've met some amazing people and done some amazing things,' said Jeff in the final show. But what he really wanted to do was head home and get to know newborn Freddy.

Dad and son bonded immediately, just as Jeff had done with Bobby 18 months earlier. 'Bobby has always been great and now there is twice the fun,' Jeff said. He already spent most weekends looking after Bobby and, if need be, was now happy to give Jade and Jackiey a break from caring for Freddie. But in the background Jade and Jeff couldn't forget that they had decided to lead separate lives and had instructed lawyers to draw up a financial settlement between them. The formal end to their love affair was in sight. Or was it?

Jade, for one, was holding out just a glimmer of hope that yet another reconciliation could be on the cards. 'Me and Jeff remind me of Kerry Katona and Brian McFadden,' she said. 'I was gutted when they split up because I think they belong together and I know that's what people think about me and Jeff too.' So what was keeping the pair apart? One big issue was the long-standing question of Jeff's alleged infidelities.

Women had been selling stories to the papers about alleged affairs since early 2003 – though in the summer of that year he attacked them as being 'absolute rubbish with no credibility'. He couldn't stop the tide, however. More rumours and press reports resurfaced the following year when Jade was pregnant with Freddy and several other women were known to have tried to sell stories about the 24-year-old to the papers.

And Jade's own hormone-fuelled insecurities about Jeff's friendships with other women led to their massive row that year, after which both had to report to their local police station for some harrowing interviews.

But, throughout all the ups and downs of their tortured relationship, Jeff has always tried to be what he is – the boy next door, the nice guy. So that's why he struggled to cope with the other rumours that he had actually hit his partner during the row.

Jade had put out an official statement through her publicist saying that Jeff had never raised a fist to her, never would, and that any stories saying he was violent were false. 'It was very unfair and just not true,' she said of the rumours.

But Jeff wanted this made even clearer. He called the papers and gave a series of 'exclusive' interviews to several newspapers on the subject. 'I want to put the record straight and tell everyone that I am not a wife-beater,' he said. 'I don't think you can ever condone a man hitting a woman. I was wrongly accused and I have been publicly humiliated.'

He was also, of course, publicly forgiven, hence his presence in the hospital for Jade's scans and for the birth itself. But that didn't stop the rumours about his wandering eye. Around the time of Freddie's birth there was talk of his closeness with stunning *Emmerdale* actress Adele Silva, with whom he had shared a bed while filming *I'm Famous and Frightened 2* for Living TV. Jeff denied a proper relationship here – and also said rumours about an affair with glamour model Jodie Marsh were equally far from the mark. 'I am sure Jodie is lovely but I think she understands that there is no way I am going to end up as one of the names on her T-shirt,' he said.

Simultaneously, in an admission that would certainly interest relationship counsellors and psychiatrists, Jade admitted that she would never have another baby – unless it was with Jeff. She also said that she couldn't stop herself from feeling jealous whenever she read about Jeff's supposed relationships with other women. 'But everyone moves on and I want Jeff to be happy,' she said quietly, when pressed about his future. Jade was determined that

Jeff would always have free and full access to his boys in the years ahead. She loved how close the three had already become and wanted them to stay friends for ever. But she knew that this meant that, if Jeff did find love with another woman, this stranger would clearly have a big role to play in Bobby and Freddy's lives. The thought of someone else changing Freddy's nappies or playing with Bobby in the park chilled her to the core, she admitted. But she was steeling herself for it one day becoming a reality.

And, while she and Jeff might no longer share a house or a bed, they were both very aware that they were all but inseparable in so many other parts of their lives. Shared screen time in television shows such as *Celebrity Wife Swap*, *Back To Reality* and *Big Brother Panto* were only one part of the equation. Further away from the public eye, they still helped run the Sunbed Shop in South Woodford – which had its first anniversary just after Jeff was crowned winner of *The Farm* and had built up a healthy client list of around 600 people.

The fact that Jade and Jeff's names were so often linked in the media also made them the perfect double act for future shows. Years ago a television reviewer said that an ideal chat show would be one jointly hosted by Jade and her mum Jackiey – a woman who he described as 'the undiluted essence of Bermondsey, whose voice could strip paint at 30 paces and whose unique dental arrangements may have inspired her daughter's original career choice'.

Today the 'Jade and Jeff Show' is a far more likely production – television insiders say it would be like

Richard & Judy but with the added spice of knowing that the two co-hosts will almost certainly be at loggerheads once the cameras have stopped rolling.

While programmes such as this were being considered by the couple's managers, Jade was busy trying to work out if she was really cut out for life as a single mum. In an interview after giving birth to Freddy, she said she didn't think many men would be brave enough to take on a mum of two with her own career and a strong personality to match.

She also denied that three men in particular had been up for the challenge. Tabloid gossip had recently linked her to Aston Villa striker Lee Hendrie, Jeff's best pal Lee Howells (a rumour that made all three friends laugh) and Blue heartthrob Antony Costa. Antony, who had met Jade met through mutual friends, lived just over the Essex border in Hertfordshire, was the right age for her and was suitably single. But both denied any romance. 'We're friends, just friends,' said Antony, while Jade said she was too busy to even think about finding love again.

She did, however, start spending time with one of Lee Hendrie's former teammates – 21-year-old soccer hunk Ryan Amoo, who had just started playing for Northampton Town. Having met through mutual friends, the two of them were anxious to try and get to know each other a bit more and had a romantic weekend away in the stylish and expensive Malmaison Hotel in Birmingham. Ryan also proved to be a big hit with Jade's boys – he was happy to help 18-month-old Bobby into his car seat after one early date, and had just found how easy it was to make Freddy smile by pulling funny faces at the baby.

The press, of course, found it hard to be entirely happy for Jade. 'Ryan Amoo is unique,' said one paper after their fledgling relationship first hit the headlines. 'He's the only man in the world who sees Amoo when he looks in the mirror, then sees another one when he rolls over in bed.' Perhaps because of this sort of ongoing mockery Jade was also determined to ensure she looked as good as possible at all times.

So, in early 2005, she checked into the private Capio Springfield Hospital in Chelmsford for the £3,000 breast enlargement she had been dreaming and talking about for more than a year. Her friend Charlene was with her when she arrived at the clinic before dawn on the day of her surgery and Jade then remained under observation in her room for two nights before being discharged. And even then the press wouldn't leave her alone. The *Sun* put a story on its front page and on page three saying that she wanted to look like Marilyn Monroe and had needed 'liposuction to trim her bulging belly and thighs' as well as a boob job. As if the inaccuracies weren't bad enough, the paper illustrated the piece with 'before' and 'after' shots with a pig's head on Jade's body and a mock 'builder's estimate' for how much it would cost to complete the fictional transformation. After putting a £9,000 price tag on liposuction to 'remove kebab belly', the paper joked that Jade would need £80,000 for 'voice lessons to change Sarf London screech into seductive lilt' and £220,000 for 'fashion and etiquette training'. The estimated completion date, the paper suggested in the pay-off line, was 2097.

Having been able to laugh these things off for so many years, Jade, in hospital, feeling vulnerable and fresh out of the operating theatre, collapsed in tears and had to be comforted by the clinic's nurses. Despite what some papers reported, the only operation Jade had actually endured had been one to make her boobs firmer, if not particularly larger. It had been far more painful than Jade had expected, so she wasn't feeling particularly good when she pulled the obligatory celebrity baseball cap on her head, tried to smile and faced the paparazzi outside the Essex hospital on the way to her car. But as well as an emotional reunion with her babysitting mum and boys to look forward to, Jade was also eagerly anticipating seeing Ryan again – though she had vowed he wouldn't see her body until the bruising had healed. In the meantime, she was prepared to head into the Shaftsbury Avenue offices of *Heat* magazine for a big photo shoot that would be turned into a seven-page special on her new look and make her the cover girl yet again.

Back at home, whether former Aston Villa man Ryan would turn out to be a firm fixture in Jade's life was still unclear. But what was clear is that the 23-year-old mum of two remained an old romantic at heart. She said that watching a best friend's wedding video one afternoon made her cry, and later confessed that she couldn't stop herself looking at engagement and wedding rings in jewellers' windows. So would she ever get to wear one herself?

Even if Jade's relationship with Ryan had faded away, everyone around her realised that it was probably too late to rekindle any flame with Jeff. So it looked as if Bobby and

Freddy would never live Jade's dream of dressing up as pageboys and following their two parents down the aisle in a fairy-tale wedding. Instead, the couple had to work out a very modern way to cope with the challenges that lay ahead. The challenges of their ever-developing careers and business interests. And the challenges of fully integrating possible new partners into their own lives and those of their children.

Living so close to each other meant it was easy to share the load and the joy of parenting. They had shared such things when they had been estranged in the past. Jade said Jeff was the first person she had called when she felt Freddy kick, even though they had been living separate lives at the time. He had been the first person she had called when she had damaged her eye in a DIY accident years earlier. And he would always be the first person she would call with good or bad news about their children for the rest of their lives.

As Jade passed the second anniversary of her arrival into the public consciousness and the *Big Brother* house, she was starting to wonder if this sort of stable, platonic relationship might actually be enough for her. All she had ever wanted was a husband, a family and to run a beauty business, she had told school friends years ago. Effectively, having two out of three wasn't bad, she thought ruefully.

Jade certainly had no problem supporting herself on her own. Good investments and a steady supply of new work meant that, having become the country's first reality-TV millionaire in little more than 18 months, Jade was just one or two big television jobs away from being crowned its first multimillionaire as well.

She was also far from lonely. Her mum was still her best friend, but she had many other pals who were just as close, and Jade was never at a loss to find anyone for a night out at a local pub, club or, as part of her extraordinary new lifestyle, a West End film première.

Most importantly of all, of course, was the fact that she also had Bobby and Freddy to look after. Motherhood had changed Jade dramatically. She still loved going out and the high life, but having children had shown Jade exactly where her true priorities lay and helped put everything in perspective. Bobby and Freddy gave her a sense of purpose and kept her smiling.

'This is a fun part of my life after some pretty rough times,' she said when asked to sum up her whole post-*Big Brother* experience. Her challenge for 2005 and beyond was to try and keep it that way.

chapter 14

Welcome To
My Salon

Jade and her family kicked off 2005 with a quiet and relaxing weekend at home. There had been no big New Year's Eve parties, so there were no hangovers to worry about. If I start the year as I mean to go on, then I'm looking forward to one of the calmest twelve months of my life, Jade thought as the Bank Holiday weekend ended. But, as it turned out, she couldn't have been more wrong. The year ahead was going to be headline-grabbing and heart-breaking in equal measure. There would be good times and very, very bad times. Jade would get through it, as she always did. But, for many weeks at a time, it would seem like pure hell.

Her first struggle was with a secret. She had been given the green light to open up her own beauty salon, the dream she had harboured since childhood. Producers from the digital channel Living TV had contacted her about this several months earlier, having read about her plans. 'If you really do go ahead and open a salon, we'd like to film it,' they told her. 'We won't interfere, we won't make you do anything differently, but we'd love to watch. And we know the viewers would as well.'

For Jade, the idea fitted like a glove. Being filmed as she went about her daily life was what had made her a star to start with. And never getting above herself and never turning down similar shows had kept her there. So she couldn't see any reason to say no – especially as her fee for making the programme would go some way towards paying for the new venture.

Experts say setting up in business is almost always more expensive than people imagine. And, if premises and top-of-the-range equipment are involved, as they would be for Jade, then the totals can easily top £100,000. Jade had made a lot of money so far. But she didn't want to throw any of it away on something that wasn't going to work. So she took a couple of business courses, away from the public eye, just to get a feel for the corporate world she was joining. And then with Living TV's backing she decided to go ahead – having promised not to breathe a word about her plans until later in the year.

The first crisis of Jade's year happened while she took a holiday just before the hard work of setting up the salon began. She took her boys, her mother and some friends for a sunshine break in Barbados. The beaches were wonderful, the sea was warm and Jade had no problem showing off her new boobs as she sunbathed or swam – good news for the British newspapers, which ran huge colour photos of them over several pages. As the group got into a Caribbean frame of mind, Jade was in for a surprise – professional boxer David Haye, one of her old school friends, was also on the island. The pair were having fun catching up when things started to go wrong. Another holidaymaker was apparently trying to take too many pictures; a row and a scuffle broke out, the police were called and in the end David was taken to court on the island. Jade went with him in support and was over the moon when he was acquitted and the charges thrown out. 'He was just sticking up for me, and I never mind when people take pictures of me. I'm a people person,' Jade told the posse of reporters who had been flown out to cover what they saw as the biggest story of the day.

Back in Britain, Jade was house-hunting – and looking after her financial future in the process. The home in Harlow that she had shared with Jeff (and was now sharing with Ryan) seemed to get smaller as her boys grew. And, despite her inner-city childhood and love of London nightlife, Jade was turning into more of a country girl. Just like Jordan, she had fallen in love with horse-riding and was thinking of buying a horse rather than just exercising other people's at her local stables. The £400,000 four-bedroom home she spotted in the far more rural Chipping Ongar seemed ideal. And Jade's incredible earning power meant she could afford to buy it without selling her old place.

'A lot of people make money out of property by renting out their old homes when they move up the ladder,' says financial expert Lee Grandin, whose company Landlord Mortgages helps them do just that. 'Your new tenants can pay the mortgage, if you have one, and you stand to benefit from any house price increases in the future. People see it as an extra pension, and by becoming a landlady Jade shows she's taking care of her long-term financial future so she'll be secure whatever happens to her other earnings.'

And security was something Jade had always craved. Which was why, when she was finally cleared to talk about it, she was being so careful about her beauty business. Several critics dismissed it as a reality-television stunt. But for Jade it was serious stuff. She wanted it to succeed. So the pressure was on and she knew that picking the right location was the vital first stop. 'I'd love to set up somewhere really flash. But I know if I was in Bond Street I would probably go bankrupt as I'd buy handbags and shoes all the time,' she admitted. And so, as grounded as ever, she picked somewhere far more down to earth: Hertford, a commuter-belt market town some 30 miles from her Essex home. And proving she hadn't lost the ability to laugh at herself Jade also decided to call the salon Ugly's.

'Do you want to be a Goody's girl?' That's the advert Jade put in her local job centre as she began recruiting. Her oldest friend Carly was on board, her mother was helping out and the workmen loved the mouthy girl who bossed them around as they kitted out the premises. Jade even showed that her grasp of finance was stronger than most people might have imagined. 'If I go in there and the builders are all drinking cups of tea, I'll be throwing their cups of tea at them,' she said on day one. 'You ain't here to drink tea. I ain't paying you VAT while you're drinking tea. But deduct the VAT and it's different, you can drink as much tea as you want then and I'll even make it for you.'

It was hard work and, as summer came, Jade had a huge new distraction. Her relationship with Ryan had hit the rocks in spectacular fashion. She had to move on – fast.

'Ryan had to be with me every minute of the day. We had only been going out a month when he wanted to marry me and have kids,' says Jade. It had got too heavy, too fast. And it was going to get worse.

Several months later, when Ryan sold his story to the *Sunday People*, there were lurid claims of him trapping Jade in her car and her house, head-locking her and sitting on her to stop her from getting away. In reality, Jade says things were less dramatic, but no less frightening. And, while he didn't ever hit her, his ring did catch her lip and make it bleed during one final confrontation.

So, after six months, she changed her locks, changed her phone numbers and tried to focus on other things. But even then fate was going to deal her a blow. The phone rang early one morning in August. It was the police – calling to say her dad, Andy, had died. He was just 42 years old. And, as the newspapers would report, it had been a squalid, tragic and lonely end. Headlines screamed about his collapse, surrounded by needles and drugs paraphernalia, in the toilet of a KFC restaurant in Dorset. 'His death has broken Jade's heart. She always believed she could change him because all she has ever wanted was a dream holiday. But the drugs had turned him into someone we didn't know any more,' said mum Jackiey.

Unable to attend the inquest, and unsure if she should go to her father's funeral, Jade cuddled up to her two young boys at home. And she spoke endlessly on the phone to Jeff as the crisis broke, reminding herself of what a true friend he could be when the heat was on. She wouldn't forget it.

As if all this wasn't bad enough, this was when Ryan's kiss-and-tell stories hit the Sunday papers. Spread out over two weekends, the text was as embarrassing as anything Jade could have imagined. The former footballer said the couple had had sex in the car park of a motorway service station, that Jade had dressed up as a saucy secretary for him, and that she was one of the noisiest lovers he had ever had. 'Jade was a great lover. I would definitely give her ten out of ten for sexual performance. She certainly knew what she was doing' was one particularly ungallant line. And, while friends told Jade that being complimented on her bedroom skills was surely better than being slated for lacking in them, she was mortified at the thought of so many people reading the story.

With so much going on, it was little wonder that Jade was feeling weak and ill by the time Ugly's finally opened. The various crises that marked the first few days made great viewing on Living TV, though as it was a minority channel the audience figures were tiny. Gazza was an early celebrity guest – he was living locally – and the first set of customers seemed to have a great, if chaotic, time. What made worrying news, however, was Jade's collapse in the salon's first month. Taken to hospital amid rumours that she might be pregnant (which she wasn't), she was kept under observation and told to slow down. But of course she couldn't. For years now, Jade's life had only one speed

– top speed. So perhaps that's why she was too distracted to pay attention to her shopping trolley and her receipt the day she did her usual weekly shop in Asda.

On that day in early October, she bought a £16 denim waistcoat from the George range. But did she pay for it?

In what the papers called 'Asda-gate', a security alarm rang out when Jade left the Harlow store. A guard approached her, found the tag in the jacket and someone at the customer-services desk removed it so she could leave more quietly. Which was when store chiefs called the police, who studied CCTV footage, spoke to checkout staff and then asked to speak to Jade. For a time, it looked as if the richest woman in reality-television history was going to be arrested for shop-lifting. But in the end the matter was dropped – and Asda revealed several of its stores immediately sold out of the jacket in question.

The one confidence booster that saw Jade through this most volatile of years was the fact that she still seemed to reign supreme in the *Big Brother* stakes. The latest series was ultimately won by Geordie dancer Anthony Hutton. And, while his antics, and those of 'mad' Craig, belly-dancing Kemal, super-intelligent Derek Laud and poor Makosi would fill endless newspaper pages at the time, none had the staying power of Jade. And, to prove it, could anyone really pick the likes of Saskia or Science out of a line-up a year later?

However, the one event in the seventh *Big Brother* which did stick in the mind looked as if it might do Jade a favour. It was the eye-popping scene involving Kinga and a wine bottle.

'She upstaged you a bit,' one reporter told Jade afterwards.

'I don't think of it as upstaging me. It was absolutely grotesque. I just felt embarrassed for her mum and dad,' Jade replied, saying she hoped Kinga's behaviour might stop programmes playing the infamous clip of her stripping off. 'Programmes haven't stopped using that clip yet but it would be nice if they did,' Jade admitted. 'If they want to show Kinga sticking a bottle up herself rather than me getting naked, then be my guest because that clip absolutely mortifies me.'

What the strip clip also did was constantly remind Jade that she needed to keep an eye on her weight. Being busy with her kids, her media work and her salon was normally enough to keep her in shape. But towards the end of 2005, she realised that she had been drinking too many fizzy drinks and snacking on too many junk-food lunches – and that she had edged back up the weight charts. Her kebab belly was back and it seemed to make a mockery of her great new boobs. She decided to do something about it. She got a trainer, Robin Knight, signed up to run the London Marathon and, in three months, she went from 11st 7lbs to 10st 7lbs, going from a size 16 to a 12 in the process. 'I thought my jelly belly would be here for life but it's really tightened up,' she said, having been asked to pose for a magazine front page and share her diet and fitness secrets with readers.

For a while, as she began her latest diet, Jade looked on the point of returning to Jeff. The pair had been close since her father's death earlier in the year. And, with her mum babysitting, they had a few evenings out together. 'I get butterflies,' Jade told friends. She was dreaming of a third child – hopefully, a girl – and had long since said she didn't want children with anyone but Jeff. But, however hard they tried to find common ground on their dates, something seemed to push them apart. 'It's frustrating when you think you want something so much but it doesn't happen,' she said when the pair resolved to remain friends. 'We tried to start afresh, we care about one another but we are too different. We can't pull it together.'

And, as 2006 got under way, the newly slim Jade was suddenly spending time with someone else. He was a budding football agent called Jack Tweedy. And he was just 18 years old – six years Jade's junior.

Friends said Jade was crazy to consider a boyfriend whose life experiences were so much more limited than hers. And she reassured them that she knew exactly what she was doing. A love affair was wonderful. But, as always, Jade knew her real priorities were elsewhere. She had her boys. Her mother. Her family, her friends, her business and her career. 'It's been years since *Big Brother* and I'm still here!' she had yelled at the press when her beauty salon opened for business. And she had no plans of going away any time soon.

chapter 15

How to Make a Million or Two

So how did she do it? How did Jade Goody, an anonymous, unknown, £15,000-a-year dental nurse from a broken home in South London, manage to change her life so dramatically? And can anyone else do the same?

Almost everyone who goes on reality-TV shows, from *Pop Idol* and the *X-Factor* to *Big Brother* and *Wife Swap*, is secretly hoping that they too can hit the jackpot, Jade-style. Celebrity watchers say that the sheer volume of 'real people' on television means it is getting harder and harder to stand out from the crowd. But they agree it is still possible to break into the big time.

A financial analysis of all the *Big Brother* contestants shows that a small number of the early ones are indeed snapping at Jade's monetary heels, showing that getting on television is a great way to make some serious money. What the latest research also shows, however, is that payments are actually lower today than they were a few years ago. The golden age of blank cheques and reality-TV millionaires might have already passed and getting in the *Big Brother* house is now no longer any guarantee of media riches.

The original cash bonanza began with *Big Brother*'s first winner – nice guy Craig Phillips, who donated his entire £70,000 prize to help pay for a transplant for family friend and Down's syndrome sufferer Joanne Harris. The former building company boss from Liverpool still hosts a selection of DIY shows such as *House Call*, *Trading Up* and *Trading Up in the Sun* for BBC One, and television agents estimate he has earned at least £180,000 to date. Interestingly enough, Craig's charitable instincts are still as strong as ever – in 2002 he ran the London Marathon and raised more than £15,000 for the Down's Syndrome Association, for example.

The winner of Series 2, Irish former air steward Brian Dowling, has also seen a big career change. He left the £12,000-a-year basic salary of his old job behind, got an agent and has since fronted a selection of shows – including doing the voice-overs for rival reality show *The Salon*. His own programme, *Brian's Boyfriends*, was heavily promoted and this, combined with his ongoing role as a presenter on ITV's *SM:tv*, is estimated to have earned him a healthy £280,000 over three years.

Jade's big rival in Series 3, Kate Lawler, is said to have collected £240,000 from magazine and newspaper stories, and was hoping to earn another £100,000 from her fitness video, 'Kate's CardioCombat' – though sales did lag well behind those of Jade's first video when they were both released in 2002. Kate has since earned a good living hosting the ill-fated morning television show *RI:SE* on Channel 4. She has also had a popular Sunday-morning slot on Capital Radio in London – something else many media people would kill for. She too makes a decent, if irregular, extra income from magazine shoots and exclusive interview, she also starred in ITV's Celebrity Wrestling alongside none other than Jeff Braziers.

Nadia Almada, the Portuguese transsexual who won Series 4 in 2004, was expected to rival Jade in the earnings race when she first left the house. Her extraordinary life story had driven the tabloids wild – but in the end she decided not to sign any exclusive deals with them and settled instead for a less eye-catching living as a constant fixture in celebrity magazines such as *Heat* in the autumn of 2004. Experts say Nadia's long-term career and earnings are still to be determined, however. She had a walk-on part in *Hollyoaks* – playing herself – shortly after finding fame and then took the now standard step of producing a fitness video, 'Latino Dance Workout with Nadia'. Unfortunately, her dream of making it in the music business – where the real money can be made – didn't look like coming off. Her first single, 'A Little Bit of Action', entered the Top 40 in its first week at just number 27 despite a fantastic video and saturation publicity. It left the Top 40 in its second week, never to return. Nadia said that, while she may release another summer single, she is unlikely to ever record an album.

Of the rest of Jade's former housemates in 2002, Alex,

her closest friend, is reported to have collected a decent £60,000 from newspaper and magazine articles about his life. He had hoped to make more out of modelling work and advertising contracts from the likes of Brylcreem when he left the house, but less real work than expected actually materialised – though he did get to spend several luxury weeks abroad while filming occasional travelogues for *Wish You Were Here*, which is pretty good compensation.

Finally, the other non-winner who hit the headlines – 'nasty' Nick Bateman, who was kicked out of Series 1 for cheating – has shown that bad publicity can still bring in rich rewards. Nick is estimated to have made around £420,000 in four years from newspaper and magazine deals, a role as narrator of *The Rocky Horror Show* and his book, *How to be a Right Bastard*. In 2004 he joined Jade in the *Big Brother Panto* house – though reports said he was earning just £5,000 for that role, compared with her extraordinary £30,000.

Interestingly enough, there has been some bad news for more recent *Big Brother* applicants who had hoped to match these earnings. Payments from tabloid newspapers sank dramatically in 2004 and experts say they may now take years to recover. One show-business agent told the *Guardian* that the *Big Brother 5* housemates were 'deluded' about their value to the papers. And leaked figures appear to back him up.

Michelle Bass and Stuart Wilson, who hogged the headlines for their supposed romance inside the house, were by far the biggest earners from the 2004 show. But media analysts say they have collected just £200,000 between them for joint interview deals – far less than Jade had made on her own two years earlier. Stuart, seen as most likely to earn a fortune modelling after the show, found even this sort of work hard to come by. After six months back in the real world, he surprised everyone by accepting a lowly paid 'work placement' post with *Big Brother* producer Endemol, where he hoped to learn more about making rather than starring in top television shows.

Art student Shell Jubin, who followed Jade's lead by stripping in front of the cameras, was estimated to be next in the Series 5 pay race. She did some glamour shots for the *Star* but is thought to have only banked around £30,000 for the task. Second-placed trainee air steward Jason Cowan is thought to have made £8,000 for his exclusive interviews, while angry Ahmed Aghil collected £7,000, and hairdresser Dan Bryan just £6,000. In 2005, the initial payments to the likes of Anthony, Makosi, Derek, Kemal and Craig were higher. But none of the housemates turned out to have any real long term earning powers.

In some cases, what former housemates miss out on in the money stakes, they gain in other areas, however. In the official *Inside Big Brother* book, television psychiatrist Sandra Scott analysed the reasons why people apply to go on the show. 'Financial gain is not the only aim,' she concluded. 'It is much more about making a mark, becoming "someone", having their 15 minutes of fame. Even though they may not make the top rank of celebrities, they are invariably higher up than they were before they went in, and they are higher up than what they consider the average person to be.'

And, while Jade is higher up than the other *Big Brother* contestants in the earnings race, even she is lagging behind the men in suits who run Britain's biggest television, telephone and entertainment companies.

Peter Bazalgette, chairman of *Big Brother* producer Endemol UK, is one of Britain's richest men, with a personal fortune running into millions. Jade's agent, John Noel, is also in the pink. His early interest in the show, when many other agents and media types were convinced it would never take off, has turned out to be a shrewd move. As well as Jade and Series 1 winner Craig Phillips, he represents high-earning presenters Davina McCall and Dermot O'Leary.

Channel 4 itself can almost be said to have been rescued from financial crisis by Jade and Co. in 2002. A year before their series began the channel had made a £20 million loss and was seeing viewing figures slide. The 2002 crowd's antics saw audiences rise by 25 per cent and enabled the channel to charge up to £100,000 per advertising slot for the final episodes. The audience share of E4, the loss-making digital channel set up to run alongside Channel 4, doubled as soon as *Big Brother 3* started showing, and the ratings for Dermot O'Leary's *Big Brother's Little Brother* show on the channel were up 200 per cent on a year before. Television analysts said the *Big Brother* effect in 2002 also boosted audiences for Graham Norton's chat show that followed it each night, and for the ailing breakfast show *RI:SE*, allowing the channel to increase advertising rates and make even more money.

Channel 4 also decided to charge for live streaming

Internet access to the show for the first time when Jade was in the house. That helped it collect an estimated £500,000 from 25,000 computer-literate subscribers. Mobile phone firm O₂ said it had processed more than 6.5 million text-message votes by the final week of the 2002 show – and, when text news updates, ring tones and logos costing between 25p and £1.50 a time were taken into account, another multimillion-pound windfall had been rung up.

Last but not least are digital votes. Even though these were in their infancy in 2002, BSkyB is thought to have made more than £1 million from interactive voting on remote-control handsets. 'If *Big Brother* were one company or product, collecting all the various revenues itself, it would be among the most profitable parts of the UK media,' said stockbroker Simon Wright, who researches media companies for British investors. 'Jade was certainly responsible for boosting Endemol's revenues by reinvigorating the *Big Brother* franchise after a poor second series. That helped cement the company's position as one of the biggest players in the British media and made everyone aware of just how useful someone like Jade can be in the battle for ratings and advertising money.

'Bearing in mind how much Jade has made for other people and other companies over the years, it seems only fair that she has done so well herself. Especially as back in 2002 she missed out on the £70,000 first prize.'

But Jade was just as busy making plenty of money for other television companies as well. Critics of her media career have attacked her for sticking incestuously to high-profile reality-based projects from the likes of Endemol.

She would be nothing without this one big backer, jealous postings in various Internet chat rooms claim.

But Endemol hasn't been Jade's only television employer. *Celebrity Driving School*, *Back To Reality* and *Celebrity Wife Swap* were all set up and put together by rival production companies. And that rivalry is intense. Behind the scenes the television world is fiercely competitive with a host of independent firms all fighting to come up with the best new formats and then bidding to get the best talent to perform in them. These companies are also tough paymasters. If they don't think a star is capable of bringing in the ratings, they will drop him or her like a stone. Like every other television personality, Jade's career is on a permanent knife-edge and every show could pretty much be her last. Of course, every show could also be her springboard into something even bigger, which is why she has had to get so good at playing the media game.

'You have to shake a lot of hands and sit through a lot of pitches if you want to get in the best shows,' says producer Liz Colbert, who has worked on several of Channel 4's blockbuster chat and reality programmes. 'Performers have to learn how to play the game. They have to look interested and show willing even when the ideas are pretty awful because they need the producers to respect them enough to call back if they ever do hit upon a winner.'

Over the years, Jade has sat through far more meetings than her relatively modest list of television credits suggests. She has shaken a lot of hands, smiled at a lot of faces and talked a lot of talk – always in the hope that the next big assignment is just one phone call away.

She has also had to sit through a lot of other meetings about her own finances. Over the years, dozens of the world's biggest entertainers claimed to have been ripped off, swindled or embezzled by dodgy agents, advisers or bankers. Jade, who had lived without money for so long, was determined not to lose the cash she had made – and financial advisers applauded her as a fantastic role model for others.

'People like Jade aren't actually as rare as you might think,' said Anna Bowes, director of Chase de Vere Investment Solutions, which helps newly rich people from all walks of life look after their money. 'Lottery winners, pop stars, footballers, even computer-game writers can see their bank balances change almost overnight, and because we don't really teach kids about money in school it can be very hard deciding what to do with it. And while it sounds crazy it is a fact that having too much money too fast can actually do you harm. You think it makes you strong but in reality it makes you vulnerable. You're a target when you suddenly hit the big time, and there are an awful lot of sharks out there ready to try and spend your money for you.'

Bowes says reports of court cases by celebrities who have been ripped off by their accountants or other advisers tend to miss one key point. 'It may feel good if you take your manager or adviser to court after you've been swindled, and if you win you may have the satisfaction of seeing him or her go to prison. But will you get your money back? And if you are in the media will your career last long enough so you can earn it all again if necessary? The crucial thing is to ensure that you have people around you that you can trust and that you make sure you know what they are doing with your money so they can't take it from you in the first place.'

Jade, hopefully, has learned that lesson well. Her first anti-shark strategy was to downplay her potential earnings – something she continues to do today. 'I've treated my mum, sorted my debts out and I'm very comfortable,' was all she would say of her early money-spinning deals immediately after *Big Brother* – a line she still uses now.

Her next plan was to take money seriously. 'I'm saving a lot. I was naïve in *Big Brother* and I'm learning more about life. I have to keep on the ball and be aware of the money I am earning and where it is all going. I'm going to get myself a flat and a car so they are mine. Then if nothing works out for me, I've still got them.'

This wasn't the attitude that many commentators had expected. Tom Lappin of the *Scotsman* newspaper said Jade's mannerisms and facial expressions in her first few days out of the *Big Brother* house were eerily familiar. 'She's Viv Nicholson, the peroxide-blonde pools winner from the 1960s, the "spend, spend, spend" girl who treated money as an impostor and made sure it was used before it could turn to dust in her hands.' The chief News International negotiator, who had bid for Jade's story in those wild, early days of freedom, was equally damning. 'This doesn't last for ever,' she warned the girl. 'Your shelf life is shorter than a pop star's.' But neither had counted on Jade's hard knocks school of money management.

'Not having had it, I wouldn't miss it,' Jade had said to

fireman Jonny about the £70,000 top prize in the *Big Brother* show, when they had been musing about who might win. 'But if I did get it then it would sort me out and I could pay off my family's debts,' she said.

After that, Jade said she would always be surprisingly cautious about money. She also proved that old habits can die hard – and that, when you have spent so much of your life struggling for every penny, you can have a strange attitude towards any new fortune you acquire.

Charles Ingram, who lived with Jade in *Celebrity Wife Swap*, said at the time, 'Jade is so stingy, even though I gather she is quite well off now. She is like the Queen – she never carries money. Once I sent her out shopping with £50 and she came back having spent £55.38. You should have heard the grief I got about her having to pay the extra.'

What Jade has also done, however, is to remember just how lucky she is to be able to go shopping at all, let alone in some of the country's most expensive stores. 'It breaks my heart when I think about how many single mums are out there doing everything that they can so that they can buy presents for their kids,' she said one Christmas after *Big Brother* had changed her life for ever. 'Then everything gets reduced to half price about a week later in the sales. Just thinking about it makes me want to cry.'

Keeping her feet on the ground by never forgetting her roots has helped Jade with more than just her money management. It has also kept her in touch with real life, and has ensured she avoids a second backlash from the media and the British public. 'Ever since she left the *Big Brother* house Jade has proved much shrewder than everyone thought,' says *Daily Express* show-business reporter Gill Swain. And we can all learn from her lessons.

In a nutshell, the experts say you need several key attributes if you are to make the leap from reality TV or talent shows into the high-earning world of mainstream entertainment. These are the things that can help the next suddenly famous face from the *X-Factor*, *Pop Idol*, *Big Brother*, *Wife Swap*, *Faking It* or any other fly-on-the-wall television show to attain more than the proverbial 15 minutes of fame. Not surprisingly, Jade has all of these key attributes in spades – and she has proved to be a master at promoting them.

Here are the 10 key qualities the experts say you need to get famous and to stay that way.

1. Be noticed – for being yourself

Reality TV and talent show contestants are 10 a penny nowadays. So the first task is to stand out from the crowd and get noticed. Regrettably, as several other *Big Brother* contestants have found over the years, you can't do this just by showing off, acting a part or trying to run the show. 'We can all spot a fake,' says PR expert and celebrity interviewer Gaynor Pengelly. 'If you are too loud just for the sake of it, then viewers will be able to tell and won't bond with you. Jade was loud because that was the kind of person she was. It was obvious from the start that we were seeing the real Jade – not least because a lot of what we saw was pretty unattractive. She wasn't putting on an act for the cameras or trying to be someone she isn't. From day one it was pretty much a case of "what you see is what you get", and people respect that and slowly they did come to like her.'

Getting noticed can happen in a host of different ways. 'Contestants in shows like *Big Brother* need to focus on making an impact, not winning,' says Tim Burrowes, editor of *Media Week*, confirming that Jade had unwittingly played the fame game perfectly while in the *Big Brother* house. 'The more controversial you are, the more newspapers are going to want your story. And any TV company that is going to give someone a job is looking for people viewers can engage with and like. The public have a very short memory and as *Big Brother* clocks up more series there will be a lot of has-beens out there.'

Other reality-TV experts say that, if you are trying to break into the big time today, you need to realise that the competition will also be tougher than ever. 'Contestants are different now. They are more media-savvy, more *Big Brother*-savvy. They are more likely to know what they want out of the experience and see themselves as going places,' says psychologist Dr Cynthia McVey from Glasgow Caledonian University. Advertising executives like to find what they call Unique Selling Points (USPs) about products to get them off supermarket shelves and into shopping trolleys, for example. It's the same with the fame game. If you are to rise above the masses, you need an edge or an attribute that no one else currently has. Interestingly enough, that edge need not have anything to do with natural talent. Caroline Buckley, the girl who left Simon Cowell speechless in the first series of *Pop Idol* with her rendition of 'YMCA', managed to carve a minor career out of that one awful performance. She was asked back to the live finals show and even ended up starring in a decently paid Pizza Hut commercial.

With Jade the USP was, surprisingly, her massive unpopularity in the first few weeks of *Big Brother*. No one ordinary member of the public had been attacked so much, or so viciously, by the British media before – especially when they were in no position to know about the attacks, let alone to defend themselves against them. The media storm was such that you didn't actually need to watch the show to know Jade's name. And that is considered to be gold dust in the fame game. The next step is to turn your USP into a solid advantage. With Jade, the fact that she had been knocked so hard and was still smiling turned her into a survivor – something else the tabloids and the celebrity world love.

Public opinion changed dramatically, from hating Jade to seeing her as a victim who needed protecting. 'She went from a pig to an underdog in one easy leap,' said one uncharitable media commentator. And she wasn't afraid to milk the part. On her first day in the *Big Brother Panto* house, in December 2004, Jade said she didn't want to be cast as an ugly sister. 'For two years of my life I was called a pig, remember?' she said.

'Well, it didn't do you any harm,' replied old friend Spencer, with just a touch of envy as he thought about all her work and all her earnings since then.

In one final piece of luck, Jade – like Madonna, Geri and Kylie – was also blessed with an unusual name that's short enough for newspaper headlines and sticks in the mind.

Amazingly enough Jade became so well known that in 2002 an Oxford University Press survey of Britain's Brainiest Kids found that a disturbingly high proportion of them thought *Little Women* and *Pride and Prejudice* had been written by that well-known 18th-century author Jade Austen rather than the real-life Jane Austen. It was a stroke of luck for Jade that her name is so unusual and memorable. But it helped.

So should anyone wanting to follow in Jade's footsteps change their ordinary name into something more exciting? Probably not. The press will find out what you've done and you'll be exposed as a fake and a wannabe – which can kill your media career stone dead. So make the most of what you do have. Nick Bateman doesn't have the most fascinating name in the world, for example, but being tagged 'nasty Nick' got him the immediate recognition that keeps his agent's phone ringing to this day.

2. Tell all

Nowadays we want to know every last detail about our favourite celebrities. And the more they have to tell us, the better. That's why newspaper and magazine staff fight for access to the most popular reality-TV and talent shows in the hope that they can sign up the winners – or the most newsworthy contestants. What they don't want, when their chequebooks are open, is to discover that the person they want to profile has had a simple, ordinary life because it's hard to make screaming headlines out of normality.

That clearly wasn't the case with Jade. Few 21-year-olds can claim to have had such a troubled or eventful past. Nor to have had such an extraordinary cast of characters within their families. From the 'jailbird dad' and the 'one-armed lesbian mum' to the 'peroxide-blonde, on-the-run grandmother' and the 'long-lost adopted brother', there was enough to write about for months. 'If Jade Goody hadn't existed, Mike Leigh would have had to invent her,' said the *Scotsman*'s Alistair McKay, referring to the British film director famous for his extraordinary and larger-than-life central characters.

And, while it may not have seemed like much fun at the time, Jade's profile was massively helped by the willingness of her friends and family to accept cash from reporters in return for their stories, memories and photographs. It is something *Big Brother* contestants are warned about during the 'talk of doom' from producers, who try to spell out the worst that can happen once you go on the show, to ensure no one can claim to have been misled about the experience.

Even so, Melanie Hill, dubbed the 'maneater' by the press in the first series of *Big Brother*, says she was horrified at the sheer number of reporters who camped outside her family home while she was inside the *Big Brother* house. 'Friends and ex-boyfriends had been hounded with lavish offers to sell their stories, but luckily for me most of my friends were loyal and supportive,' she says. That kept Mel's privacy intact, which is exactly what she wanted. But it wouldn't have been the right thing if she had wanted a lucrative media career at any cost.

In 2004 *Big Brother*'s eventual winner Nadia Almada also took a different approach to the media when she was released from the house. As a transsexual she was deeply worried about the way the 'red-top' tabloids might treat her particularly sensitive story, so she decided not to conduct any newspaper interviews on the night of her eviction. 'She was nervous and a bit concerned that her story was not to be told in a sensational way and that there would not have been an opportunity to turn something more considered around,' said Catherine Lister, who was handling Nadia's interview requests for her new agents John Noel Management.

In the end Nadia decided to give her story – and more time to write it – to *Heat* magazine. But insiders say she probably made little more than £30,000 or so in the process. That is a lot of money for the former department-store perfume seller. But it is a fraction of what Jade had earned by trusting the tabloids two years earlier.

Finally, it also pays to admit your own mistakes and shortcomings. Today's biggest stars are our most human ones – the people we can all identify with and who we can see struggling with the same demons we all face every day. As Geri Halliwell says, 'The way forward is to show your imperfections. To admit, "I don't really know what I'm doing, but I'm trying."' Mark Frith, editor of *Heat* magazine, says this simple humility and honesty is what readers want to see. The most inspiring stars are the most approachable, and carry with them the perfect mixture of the ordinary and the extraordinary. Jade practically defines that description. And that is what keeps us all clamouring for more.

3. Be good at what you do

Fortunately, you don't need to have any particularly extraordinary talents to stay in the public eye. Being a good guest on chat shows sounds too simple to be true, but it works. Anyone who saw Michael Parkinson squirm when, in 2004, Hollywood star Meg Ryan refused to answer any of his questions with more than a few short words will appreciate that other chat-show producers are unlikely to give her any more publicity by rushing to get her on their stages. Graham Norton, however, has said guests such as comedienne and radio presenter Sandi Toksvig are so easy to talk to, and so naturally funny, that they will always be called upon to appear on his show at the last minute if others cancel their appearances. That keeps Sandi in the public eye and helps her sell more books and win more vital publicity for her radio shows and other work.

Jade's ebullient style was probably what persuaded Paul O'Grady to have her on his afternoon chat show as the *I'm A Celebrity – Get Me Out Of Here* correspondent in November 2004. He, and his audience, knew Jade would be giggly, gossipy and good fun when she came on to discuss the show. She delivered, and made one of the shows even more memorable when she came on stage with toddler Bobby in her arms and proudly showed him off to the audience. This sort of value for money means she's pretty much guaranteed to be asked back in the future.

4. Be nice to everyone you meet

Acting like a prima donna can sound great fun – and can produce some great headlines, as J-Lo and her allegedly huge entourage and list of requests before she agrees to any live or television performance can attest. But being rude or overly demanding can make you enemies when what you need, if you are going to make it in the media, are good friends. The unlikely friendship between 23-year-old Jade and 49-year-old Lily Savage creator Paul O'Grady is a good example. The pair met when filming *Celebrity Driving School* for Comic Relief. They got on well and they stayed in touch. Now, because they enjoy each other's company, they can help each other out. Hence, Jade's role on Paul's chat show when she was looking for a relaxed way back on to our television screens after Freddy was born in 2004. If Jade had acted the big star and refused to mix with everyone on *Celebrity Driving School*, she would never have made this connection. Being nice isn't just free. In the fame game it can be invaluable and it's a great investment for the future.

Genuine kindness will always be recognised by others as well – even your rivals. Christine Hamilton is one of the many 'famous for being famous' names who competes for the kind of television roles that Jade normally wins. But she has nothing but praise for her competitor. 'I don't think there is a nasty bone in Jade's body. She survived the monstering that she got by the press and she's turned it around and made a very good career out of being Jade Goody – and good luck to her.'

Other stars say that you never know who might be your next co-star, so again it pays to take the time to get to know everyone you can. Before he took on the role of wide boy Dennis Rickman in *EastEnders*, for instance, actor Nigel

Harman played one of the leading roles in the Abba musical *Mama Mia*. He shared a few jokes every night with his make-up girl at the Prince Edward Theatre in London. And it was a good job that he did, because years later that make-up girl, Jessie Wallace, would join him in Albert Square when she took on the role of Kat Slater. Show business is a notoriously small world, so the nicer you are to everyone, the easier the profession will be. Jade was called 'an absolute sweetie' by the staff on *Celebrity Driving School*, even though she was dealing with her tempestuous personal life and a stressful pregnancy at the time. Her good attitude would continue to pay off for years to come.

5. It takes two

There's Posh and Becks, Madonna and Guy and, until recently, there has been Kerry and Brian, and Jennifer and Brad. Celebrity couples don't necessarily make twice the headlines and bank twice as much cash as their single rivals. But having a famous other half brings several key benefits – as Jade and Jeff have found.

First, you can share the profile so you never bore the public. *Heat* magazine was happy to put Jade on the cover for an amazing five weeks in a row in the spring of 2004. Six would probably have been overkill – so Jeff went on the cover a few weeks later instead under the headline: 'Has Jeff got a new girlfriend?' (The answer, by the way, was no.)

Jeff, of course, also provided more interest to Channel 5's *Back To Reality* when he was introduced to the house as a surprise mystery guest in 2004, making Jade the only housemate to have her partner there as a confidante and supporter. Jeff also added spice to the coverage of the *Big Brother Panto* at the end of 2004 and the start of 2005 by co-hosting Channel 4's daytime coverage of it with June Sarpong – and keeping Jade on her toes.

In a nutshell, a celebrity couple provides a form of 'buy one, get one free' offer to broadcasters, newspapers and magazines – though in Jade and Jeff's case, both collect healthy fees for their individual services. However, a final word of warning. Fake relationships won't work. The ups and downs Jade and Jeff have experienced over the years have been honest and heartfelt, and fans appreciate this. When two famous names appear to get together simply to win more headlines then the public smells a rat and both sides can lose out.

6. Never forget your roots

Soap stars do it all the time and fall flat on their faces. They leave the shows that made them famous, determined to move into television drama in Britain or even films in Hollywood. *Coronation Street*'s Sarah Lancashire, *EastEnders*' Michelle Collins and *Brookside*'s Sue Johnston and Ricky Tomlinson have all successfully made the first leap. Very few have followed them and fewer still have made it as film stars.

The lesson, media experts say, is never to try moving too far from the things that got you famous in the first place. Jade has never made this mistake. She keeps her names in newspapers and magazines by becoming a commentator on subsequent series of *Big Brother* or other reality-TV shows such *as I'm A Celebrity – Get Me Out of Here*. She happily appears in reality-TV spin-offs herself – from *Back To Reality* to *Big Brother Panto*.

And she never lets it all go to her head. 'Jade has done so well because she has handled everything with a mixture of sense and humility,' says *Daily Express* writer Gill Swain. 'That's how she's avoided falling into the mantraps of vanity, arrogance and pretension, which yawn at the feet of many who suddenly have fame thrust upon them.'

It's something Jade realised very early on – when she was determined never to make those who have not done as well as her feel bad. Soon after leaving the *Big Brother* house and making some decent money for the first time in her life, Jade decided to learn to drive and buy a car. But, while she had a bit of fun wandering around some top-of-the-market showrooms, she was too sensitive to go completely crazy. 'I don't want anything too flashy,' she said finally. 'I don't want people thinking, Oh my God, she's been on television and now she's got a flashy car. That wouldn't be the real me.'

And the real Jade Goody was what the public always wants to see. The people who book guests on to chat shows and place interviews with them for newspapers say Jade is still the top of many lists because she hasn't tried to confuse or alienate her fans by pretending to be something she isn't.

'When you are famous for something, you should stick to it and play to your strengths,' says celebrity public relations expert Gaynor Pengelly. 'If you want to move on, you need to do it very slowly and gradually so you make sure you bring your fans with you. Trying to leap too fast from one type of role to another can be confusing and you can end up in no-man's-land.' It's the problem the Spice Girls faced and the problem Charlotte Church and almost every boy band are still facing. You might be growing up yourself and want to be taken more seriously, or go in a different direction, but your fans might just want what you have always given them – and will disappear if you offer something different.

Early on in her fame Jade admitted that she couldn't really sing – and wouldn't try to make it as a pop star. As fellow *Big Brother* contestant Nadia found out in 2004, this was a wise move. A hit record can transform your career forever – just ask former *Neighbours* actress Kylie – but a flop can make you look desperate and end your whole career.

That's why Jade has never shied away from returning to her reality-TV roots – writing *Big Brother* commentary columns, talking about *I'm A Celebrity – Get Me Out of Here!* on chat shows and getting back into *Big Brother*-type situations whenever required.

She has also worked incredibly hard to make this celebrity niche her own. As her soon-to-be agents John Noel Management said the moment Jade left the *Big Brother* house in 2002, 'There is only one Jade Goody.' She is determined to keep it that way.

7. Grab free training when it's offered

Veteran disc jockey Dave Lee Travis is no fan of Jade, or any other reality-TV contestants. 'The world has been taken over by people like Jade. Total non-entities who have no talent for anything whatsoever,' he said critically. But Jade, at least, has never pretended to be anything that she's not. She has also been prepared to learn whatever skills it takes to stay in the public eye and to win all her jobs on merit. As well as taking private tuition to improve her reading and writing, over the years Jade has also become a decent dancer. She has been happy to listen to the experts and drill away at new routines until the moves look good enough. She's also been prepared to take whatever free instruction has been on offer. She admitted that part of the appeal of *Big Brother Panto* was that it would give her the chance to work with some of Britain's best writers, directors, acting coaches and choreographers. The fact that she would be on camera while she got the experts' advice – or faced their criticism – wasn't a problem for her. The key was to learn a little more about the entertainment business and become a more confident, capable and rounded performer in the process.

If you want to move your career on, it is also worth remembering the old rule that if you don't ask you don't get. So if your profile is high enough you may as well use it to pitch for your dream job. Jade did just that in early 2005, when she followed up an earlier comment and told a celebrity magazine how much she wanted a bit part in *The Bill*. 'I know this sounds silly but at some point I'd love to try my hand at acting,' she told *OK!* magazine. 'I'd love to be in *The Bill*. Even if it's just for one episode, so I can wear a copper's outfit. So if anyone is reading this, please let me be in *The Bill* for one episode.'

To date we don't know if anyone in the show's production department has made the call. But, whatever else Jade is accused of, you can't say she's afraid of putting herself forward for things. Then you have to give her the credit for the times she succeeds.

Finally, it is worth remembering that all publicity is good publicity. Off-the-wall chefs David Myers and Simon King were not being particularly gallant in BBC Two's cookery show *The Hairy Bikers' Cookbook* when they made cabbage soup. 'It's a lovely colour. It looks like jade,' said David as he stirred the pot. 'I hope you mean jade the stone and not the fat bird from *Big Brother*,' replied his companion. And reminding us all of how Jade used to look was no bad thing when that particular insult was aired – because Jade herself was all over ITV looking fantastic and advertising her latest diet and weight-loss programme for *OK!* magazine at the same time.

8. Put the hours in

A few photo shoots, a magazine interview, a great new television project. The modern celebrity lifestyle can sound fantastic. But experts say famous people are like ducks – they look serene and calm on the surface, but they're exhausting themselves by paddling away like crazy underneath.

An appearance on a kids' television show on a Saturday or Sunday morning can mean you never get a day off, for instance. And, while appearing on *GMTV* or any other breakfast show can look good fun, it won't always feel that way when you are told you need to get to the studio by 4 a.m. so you can talk to the producers, get in make-up and be on set at 6 a.m. It is also worth remembering that, for every one appearance, job or project fans are aware of, celebrities have probably done the work on at least three others. The treadmill rarely even slows down when you are trying to stay in the public eye.

Jade, fortunately, is always prepared to go the extra mile, when necessary, to push her career forwards. 'I've always worked hard for my money. I'm stupid, to be fair, but I've always been ready to go out to work,' Jade said after her first million had been made. And that work sometimes felt as if it never stopped.

'In this business you sometimes have to be prepared to put your relationships and social life on hold,' says American actor Mark Setlock, who gives up six nights a week to appear in West End shows such as the celebrity-focused hit *Fully Committed*. 'And while you may only work the standard eight hours in any given day, the piecemeal way your work is structured means that these eight hours may be spread over a 12-hour period or longer. However tired you are, if an art director wants one more hour of photographs then you pretty much always have to agree.'

Then, of course, come the more serious sides to life in fame's fast lane. 'Every step celebrities take nowadays is usually accompanied with a legal contract,' says entertainment lawyer John Ireland, whose recent celebrity clients have included Miriam, the transsexual star of Sky's reality show *There's Something About Miriam*. 'The show-business world is full of pitfalls and, from the terms and conditions of a television show to the newspaper exclusive, you need to get legal advice before signing anything. People like Jade will have to spend time finding legal advice they can trust and will need regular meetings with their advisers to ensure their interests are always being protected. That's the less glamorous but equally important side of being famous, but it is something you do have to get used to.'

9. Take control of your own image

That's exactly what Jade has done. In the awful early days after *Big Brother* she saw how desperate the media was for even the smallest scrap of information about her life. And she saw how friends and even some family members were able to cash in and sell facts, photographs and even pure fiction to various newspapers and magazines.

When all that had ended, and when Jade's own life was back on an even keel, she decided to play the media at its own game – by staying in complete control of her image and her life story. To this day Jade is the one who decides what the outside world should know about her. She picks the large and small events she is prepared to share with others. She picks up the phone to pass on the stories and agree to the pictures. Most importantly, she gets to pick up the cheques.

Amazingly enough, selling just an exclusive cover story to a celebrity magazine or newspaper every few months can easily produce a healthy income of more than £100,000 a year, according to show-business agents. And, if you control the stories, you can ensure that you don't ever get taken by surprise by some awful revelations, and that you are almost always shown in a sympathetic light. So Jade can let the cameras in on all the good occasions – birthdays, Christmas dressing-up parties, shopping trips, sunshine holidays. It's fun and it's lucrative. But it isn't always as simple as it looks. Too many soft stories and people will get bored. Too few and they may forget who you are. So far, Jade has been the queen of this tricky balancing act.

Jade has also proved to be particularly adept at knowing when to raise her public profile. On 7 December 2004, for example, you would have expected the papers to be full of stories of ITV's *I'm A Celebrity – Get Me Out of Here* show, which had ended amid massive publicity the previous night. Squeaky-voiced comedian Joe Pasquale had beaten Paul Burrell and Fran Cosgrave into second and third place to win the series, and you would have imagined his face to be all over the press the following day. But who popped up instead, to dominate the *Sun*'s gossip columns in not one but six large colour photographs? None other than Jade Goody, of course, out on the town and happily hamming it up for the paparazzi in London's celebrity haunt the Attica club.

10. Have fun

Jade says she was almost addicted to celebrity television shows when she was a child in Bermondsey. She loved glittering awards ceremonies and star-studded variety shows. She dreamed of one day being there herself – and now she is loving every minute of it. 'Everyone has a dream and I'm living mine,' she says, fully aware of how lucky she is. And that, celebrity experts say, is important as well. They say people who seek fame and enjoy fortune soon lose their appeal if they are forever talking about how hard their lives have become and how tough it is being famous, beautiful or desirable. Staying humble and being grateful pays dividends.

But, once more, you need to be genuine. And Jade certainly is, silently thanking her lucky stars every time the phone rings with another offer of work. 'I didn't expect to be this busy,' she told *Now* magazine at the end of 2004. 'I'm still really surprised and chuffed when people want to get me on telly or ask me to get involved in something. I know I'm very lucky.'

Jade is also willing to give things back to causes that mean a lot to her. In the very early days of her fame, when she was preparing to star in pantomime in Gravesend, Kent, she was contracted to visit a series of local hospitals to meet some patients and drum up some publicity. But those visits turned into more than just a job for the 21-year-old. Friends said she found visiting the children's wards in the run-up to Christmas particularly emotional. So she has quietly worked for several children's charities ever since.

Often Jade picks organisations that are essential to many youngsters' well-being, but are almost entirely overlooked. Take lollipop people – men and women who protect kids on the way to and from school in all weathers, all through the year. 'It is becoming increasingly difficult to recruit lollipop people because their profile is so low,' said Penny Sczcepaniak, communications manager of motor firm Hyundai, which decided to try and boost public awareness of them with an awards lunch in 2003. 'We want to celebrate lollipop people and give them a little of the recognition they deserve.'

Jade's arrival at the ceremony helped do just that. After dressing up in the bright-yellow lollipop uniform for a photo call in central London, she was also happy to stay around after the awards were handed out, to thank every volunteer she met. 'When Bobby grows up and goes to school I hope that he will be looked after by someone as caring and committed as the lollipop people here today,' she said afterwards.

Having had such a tough childhood herself, it is little surprise that Jade was also happy to be the face of kids' charity Barnardo's annual Big Toddle walk, which raises cash to help vulnerable children under the age of five. Jade, who said she nearly died of fright as a teenager when she did a bungee jump to raise money for a breast cancer charity, has continued to turn up at key charity events ever since. After watching the awful events in South-East Asia unfold on television over Christmas 2004, Jade said she was more than happy to tackle her first ever live radio broadcast to try and raise funds for the tsunami victims as part of UK Radio Aid. She co-hosted a show with Classic FM's Simon Bates, and shared the bill with the likes of Zoe Ball, Shane Ritchie, Chris Evans, Kate Thornton, and old pals Davina McCall and Dermot O'Leary.

That said, Jade is far from averse to the glitzy side of fame. She is a fixture on the opening-night circuit and gets her mum or Jeff to babysit while she goes clubbing at some of London's most exclusive venues – often being photographed falling out of them in the early hours after letting her hair down just that little bit too much. 'Fame has allowed me to do a lot of things that otherwise I wouldn't have done. I get to go to celebrity events, different places. It's given me a hell of a lot, and I will appreciate all of it for as long as it lasts,' she said.

chapter 16

Jade's World

Following in Jade's footsteps won't be easy for any future Big Brother or other reality-TV participant. But in some ways Jade sees that the biggest example she can set for others has nothing to do with either fame or fortune. Her key message is that, if you believe in yourself, have sound family values and good friends, then you can withstand almost anything that life can throw at you. It is something that Jade has proved more comprehensively than almost anyone else in the public eye today. And Jade has also shown that where you start in life should always count for far less than where you end up.

Jade Goody has certainly been on an incredible journey. Not just from a broken home, but from a broken home with so many other stresses, strains and pressures that could have easily seen her follow a path towards the very bottom rung of the social ladder. Crime and drugs were in the streets all around her as a child, and the temptations to take them, or to try and make money out of them, must sometimes have felt intense. But Jade has never wavered in her opposition to drugs and all the social problems they cause.

Hard work, good luck and sheer determination have helped give her the means to take herself away from the mean streets of her childhood. But along the way Jade has never forgotten who she is or where she comes from.

For all their ups and downs, Jade's mum Jackiey remains her closest confidante, supporter and friend. And Jade has identified her true priorities in life. 'I may not be the brightest girl around but I know that I'm a good mother and that's the most important thing to me. I've never known happiness like you feel when you see your child smile,' she said after Bobby was born. It was a lesson she swore never to forget, and it was one she learned afresh when Freddy was born in the autumn of 2004.

For her own part, *Big Brother*'s baby was forced to grow up fast when she came out of the house and realised just how savagely every part of her appearance and her life had been attacked by the media. Finding out that the country's best-selling papers – the ones you yourself read every day – have called you the 'most hated woman in Britain' would be enough to make most people want to hide away for the rest of their lives. Discovering that people you have never met are prepared to travel miles to jeer you on live television would hurt even more.

Jade, amazingly, has had the courage to laugh about the attacks and to forgive the individual attackers. She has picked herself up off the floor every time life has thrown her down, and she has managed to build herself the kind of life she never thought would be possible. 'I'm just a girl who went into a house and got lucky,' she said modestly when asked to sum up her life. But all the evidence says that she is far, far more than that.

Since leaving the *Big Brother* house Jade has made a million pounds and she now looks a million dollars. But she has never forgotten where her real priorities lie. So new television projects and new work commitments can come and go – for the next few years Jade's true focus will be on her children. 'I've got my boys, and that's all I care about,' she said when asked about her future. 'I make sure I treasure every single day. I want to be a perfect mum and I don't mind what people say about me. As long as the boys grow up thinking I'm a good mum then that's all that matters.' That's one reason why the end of her two-year relationship with Jeff is turning out to be far less tempestuous than much of the relationship itself. If the pair can't be a model couple, then Jade is determined to ensure they are still model parents.

When she was in the *Big Brother* house, Jade's critics said she represented everything that was bad about Britain's young people. In the years that followed, the girl from Bermondsey has managed to prove that she in fact represents the exact opposite. She has earned her own money, put her family first and shown that, if you believe in yourself, there is no limit to what you can achieve. Jade's world may not always be perfect. But it is an exciting, surprising and inspiring place. And Jade's right to be proud of it.